There is scarcely a person without sexual or social problems. Those who suffer from insomnia, impotence, frigidity, claustrophobia, overweight, stuttering, hypochondria, alcoholism, or shyness almost always want to be helped.

In earlier times, people consulted witch doctors, the stars, sorcerers, theologians, phrenologists. Then Freud introduced psychoanalysis, which acquired a reputation as a more scientifically effective way to solve life's problems.

There is another source of help now—for those who do not have the time, the money, or the inclination to seek help on the analyst's couch; a revolutionary new approach called "behavior therapy." Instead of delving deep into the unconscious to investigate and resolve conflicts taking place there, the behavior therapist cures the symptoms that result from inappropriate learning. What has been learned wrong can be "unlearned" and then set right through quick-working methods which enable the patient to help himself.

Help Without Psychoanalysis tells what behavior therapy is and what it can do for the individual who wants a proven shortcut for solving his problems.

Help Without Psychoanalysis

BY *Herbert Fensterheim, Ph.D.*

ASSISTANT PROFESSOR OF PSYCHIATRY AND CO-DIRECTOR OF THE BEHAVIOR
THERAPY TRAINING PROGRAM, NEW YORK MEDICAL COLLEGE

WITH *Lawrence G. Blochman*

STEIN AND DAY/*Publishers*/New York

FIRST STEIN AND DAY PAPERBACK EDITION, 1975

First Published in 1971
Copyright © 1971 by Herbert Fensterheim and Lawrence G. Blochman
Library of Congress Catalog No. 76-150253
Printed in the United States of America
Stein and Day/*Publishers*/Scarborough House,
Briarcliff Manor, New York 10510
ISBN 0-8128-1806-7

TO *Jean*

CONTENTS

1

AN EFFECTIVE SHORTCUT
FOR SOLVING PERSONAL PROBLEMS

THE MANY OBSTACLES lying along the road to a serene existence—fears, anxieties, and tensions—are not only universal,
but probably date back to the most primitive societies.
Even the troglodyte must have feared the unexplored dark-
ness of a strange cave.

The person with problems in today's complex society is
not unique, to say the least. He (or she) may be afraid of
dogs, airplanes, women, or his boss. He may have problems
with sexual, social, or business relations. His hangup may
be insomnia, impotence, claustrophobia, overweight, stuttering, hypochondria, bed-wetting, alcoholism, or agoniz-
ing shyness. Whatever it is, he may seek help from a
number of sources, among them a relatively recent and
revolutionary way of coping with life's problems: behavior
therapy.

Before defining behavior therapy, let us look briefly at
the way people have struggled with their psychological
problems in previous eras. Among primitive societies the
same mysterious natural forces that caused thunder and
lightning, droughts, failures of the hunt, infertility, and un-
explained death were blamed for everything unpleasant
or harmful. These forces had to be propitiated by animistic
rituals, animal sacrifices, and the consumption of hallucina-
tory plants considered sacred.

In medieval western culture, the human state depended

upon the outcome of the struggle between the transcendental forces of good and evil. Evil forces could invade and possess a man's body and change his behavior. Mental illness, on the increase during the twelfth century, was called "witch sickness" or "fiend sickness," and there were standard techniques for its treatment. The evil had to be exorcised, of course, by the laying on of hands, by the drinking of wine in which sacred objects had been washed, or by other means. Relatives suffering from witch sickness were turned out of the family residence before they could contaminate it.

Toward the end of the eighteenth century, Franz Josef Gall, a Viennese physician, devised a new method for looking at man's strengths and weaknesses. The human brain, he declared, was divided into thirty-five faculties which governed a person's mental development and character traits, such as sexuality, intelligence, industry, and sociability. Where one faculty was overdeveloped, a slight bulge appeared on the skull corresponding to the brain area involved. Underdevelopment showed a corresponding concavity in the skull. Dr. Gall called his system phrenology, and its popularity swept across the Continent like an epidemic. In the mid-1800s, phrenology was regarded as a scholarly and respected science, solidly based on contemporary research. There were more phrenologists practicing in European capitals per capita than there are psychoanalysts in most cities today.

By the turn of the century, phrenology had lost most of its followers. Scientists turned with increasing interest to the area of physics, exploring the vast cosmic forces that were keeping the universe in running order. In the midst of this revolutionary development, which seemed to dwarf the importance of the individual man, some scientists were nevertheless more interested in studying the individual, his personality and his behavior. One such man was another Viennese physician, Sigmund Freud.

Like his contemporaries, the physical scientists, Dr. Freud attempted to explain the human personality in terms of omnipotent cosmic forces. His concept, greatly simplified, was that behavior was determined by the interplay of all-powerful forces and their conflict in the unconscious. We as individuals were at the mercy of these unknown, perhaps unknowable, forces that were part of our biological essence. Yet he believed that the human intellect, through careful study, could begin to formulate the laws governing these forces. He worked out techniques through free association, dream analysis, and the transference relationship between a person and his analyst, by which these forces could be understood. For instance, he formulated systematic patterns which the forces followed, and determined their development at various age levels, designating them as the oral, anal, and genital stages. Understanding these patterns helped the individual gain insight into the conflict being waged in his unconscious. By establishing an equilibrium between the warring forces, thereby freeing him from their irrational control, he could lead a normal, healthy life.

Freud himself did not consider his psychoanalytic techniques definitive. Although much of the basic theoretical framework remained fixed, he constantly revised and reformulated his ideas, and his disciples, including his daughter Anna, have continued this process of re-examination.

The development of psychoanalysis in the early years of the twentieth century paralleled trends in the growth of modern medical sciences. Physicians began to regard symptoms as unimportant in themselves, significant only as clues to the patient's real trouble. A fever was not an illness to be treated, but rather an indication of an infection caused by some bacteria, to be eliminated from the blood-stream or the part of the body where the damage was being done.

Psychoanalysis follows this medical model. Freudians regard symptoms as important only insofar as they throw light on the underlying forces causing the neurotic be-havior. One of my training analysts used to declare: "One of the few things we can really be sure of is never to treat a symptom."

It is on this point that behavior therapy breaks sharply with psychoanalysis.

The behavior therapist *does* treat symptoms because symptoms are the form of human behavior. If they add up to neurotic behavior it is not because of unresolved un-conscious conflicts, but because of inappropriate learning. The behavior therapist believes that whatever has been improperly learned can be unlearned and replaced by a more suitable behavior pattern.

Scientifically, behavior therapy derives not from Freud but from the laboratories of Ivan Pavlov, and later of B. F. Skinner. Pavlov's dogs, having learned to associate the ringing of a bell with the appearance of meat, salivated at the sound of the bell even when the meat was not forth-coming. When the meat failed to appear for a period of time, the sound of the bell no longer produced salivation. In other words, learning is a two-way street. A dog can be conditioned to respond to a stimulus, and he can be con-ditioned *not* to respond to the same stimulus. Humans, too, can respond or not to a given stimulus. Behavior therapy is largely based on this premise.

In a few words, behavior therapy may be defined as the psychological process whereby bad habits may be changed or new and appropriate ones established.

The term "behavior therapy"—which is a relatively new concept—to describe the therapeutic application of the conditioned reflex has been variously credited to B. F. Skinner and Arnold Lazarus in the United States and H. J. Eysenck in England. One of the earliest recorded case histories dates back to 1924, when Mary Cover Jones undertook to change the behavior of a three-year-old boy who had been frightened by a white rat and whose fears had generalized to include all furry things. Dr. Jones used learning procedures to rid the boy of his fears.

Most of the major work in behavior therapy—perhaps 90 percent of it—has been done since 1960. The methodology is still taking shape at such centers as the Institute for Psychiatry at the University of London and the Temple Medical College in Philadelphia. Research is being carried on at such diverse points as Boston College and the University of California. In the New York City area the subject is being taught at the New York Medical College, Columbia University, and the State University of New York at Stony Brook, Long Island.

The behavior therapist is an empiricist. He attacks specific problems as they exist in the present. The history of the patient may be of some use if it can furnish clues to improper learning, but the therapist does not dig for childhood experiences as an indication of hidden conflicts. He is interested in what the patient is doing wrong, in the neurotic behavior that the patient wants to change. Often the problem can be stated in a simple declarative sentence: "I can't sleep nights" or "I'm afraid to ride in elevators." Sometimes his problem behavior is somewhat more complex. In all cases, however, inappropriate learning has taken place at some point, and the behaviorist therapist has techniques for its correction.

For therapeutic purposes, irrational behavior has been divided into four general groups, each requiring special treatment.

1) *The phobias.* Here the patient has learned to asso-

ciate an emotion, such as fear or anger, with an object, situation, or action. His phobia may be fear of airplanes, criticism, rejection, or sex. Just as Pavlov's dogs were conditioned to salivate at the ringing of a bell, the patient has learned, for example, to associate fear with the mere sight of an airplane. The phobia is treated in the same general way Pavlov stopped his dogs from salivating: he continued to ring the bell without producing meat. With a phobic patient we present the fear stimulus—the plane, a snake, a woman—without anxiety. The patient experiences the situation in his imagination over and over again, until it is drained of all anxiety. The technique, called systematic desensitization, is described in detail in Chapter 3.

2) *Lack of assertion.* The nonassertive person is one who cannot express his innermost thoughts and feelings openly and honestly. He is the henpecked husband, the wife with a domineering mother-in-law, the junior executive who is afraid to ask for a raise. The techniques of dealing with this problem—behavior rehearsal for assertive actions, for instance, or training in the use of language that will reveal true feelings—is to be found in Chapter 4.

3) *Persistence of undesirable habits.* What are roughly classed as undesirable habits cover a wide scope, from sexual aberrations through alcoholism to compulsive gambling. The behavior therapist regards these habits as the results of inappropriate learning, and tries to change them by creating unpleasant or even painful associations. Electric shock is among the aversive techniques that have been found useful (Chapter 6).

4) *Lack of desirable habits.* Failure to have learned simple social skills may lead to unhappy consequences. Harvard's B. F. Skinner is responsible for the technique of modifying behavior by means of rewarding the acquisition of good habits, just as he taught his rats to push levers in

order to produce food. His "operant methods" have been proved useful in establishing desirable study and work habits, and especially in treating seriously disturbed schizophrenics (Chapter 9).

Patients who have spent some years in psychoanalysis frequently find it difficult to adjust to the empirical approach of behavior therapy. They ask pertinent questions which deserve pertinent answers.

Q. Was Freud wrong? Is there no such thing as significant childhood experience? Are there no inner psychic conflicts between the id and the superego, no Oedipal situations, no instincts?

A. Freudian theory may very well be sound as a whole or in part. Behavior therapists have not tested Freud's concepts because they are irrelevant to reflex conditioning. Pavlov and Skinner and their followers were and are concerned only with here-and-now behavior and the means of modifying it. Childhood experiences may provide clues to help the behavior therapist in his diagnosis, but hidden forces in conflict are not a basis for either diagnosis or treatment.

Q. Does the transference phenomenon occur in behavior therapy?

A. This depends on the case and on the individual patient. As a rule, however, there is no transfer of unconscious childhood emotions to the therapist, something which *does* occur as an important stage in psychoanalysis. Behavior therapy can be quite impersonal, particularly when some of the operant methods are used in treating a patient. Many of its techniques depend on tape recorders, mechanical aids, and visual devices, which the patient may use at home without the presence of the therapist. The therapist acts as the expert in a co-worker relationship, rather than in the traditional parent-child relationship. The patient takes an active part in his own treatment, even when he is lying with his eyes closed, trying to relax. I don't think we reach the great depths of emotion that are often involved in psychoanalysis. Warm feelings frequently develop between therapist and patient, but they are not central to the treatment.

Q. Do you often find patients who seek behavior therapy resistant?

A. No. One man was referred to me by a Freudian-oriented colleague with the warning that he was so resistant to analysis that further sessions were useless. I had some trouble with the technical problem of relaxing him at the first session, but I recorded the exercises and gave him the tape to play at home. At the second session, he said he had not done his homework. We went through the relaxing routine again. The third and fourth sessions were the same story. He had not practiced the exercises at home. I told him that it made no difference to me whether he went through the relaxing series at home or in my office, but that he could save time and money by working with the tape between sessions. He stopped being resistant.

Q. What about symptom substitution? Isn't it true that if you rid the patient of one symptom without treating the underlying cause, either another symptom will take its place or the same symptom will reappear later in an aggravated form?

A. Behavior therapists are very much interested in the problem of symptom substitution and are currently studying the matter clinically and experimentally. The evidence to date indicates that the appearance of another symptom or the later reappearance of the same symptom is a very rare phenomenon, which may have been caused by situations not at all related to the problem the therapist and the patient are dealing with. In general, when a symptom is removed, the patient is better able to cope with future problems.

In a recent experiment conducted with a number of New Haven children aged nine and ten, all bed-wetters, 80 percent of the children getting therapy (the method is described in Chapter 9) conquered their enuresis in ten weeks. There was no change in the control group. A follow-up check found no new symptoms and no unfavorable personality changes. Other studies have furnished similar evidence.

In addition to a different approach to symptoms, behavior therapy differs from psychoanalysis in the time required to produce results. Years may pass before the patient undergoing psychoanalysis is able to bring the conflicting forces within him to the surface of his consciousness. Behavior therapy requires much less time. Averaging a mixed bag of neuroses from the phobias through depressions and compulsions, most cases can be helped in from twenty to forty weekly sessions. Some are resolved in three or four sessions. With some others, behavior therapy doesn't work at all. In my own experience, however, nearly 70 percent of those who come for consultation are helped.

Those whom behavior therapy cannot help are usually recognizable during the first few sessions. Often they do not want to change their behavior because they find their neuroses rewarding. But to blame all failures on the patient would be to deny the truth of Dr. Joseph Wolpe's dictum: When the patient is not getting any better, the therapist is doing something wrong.

Nothing is more rewarding to a therapist than to find that he has done something right, and that the conditioned reflex is indeed the key to unlocking personality potentials. Because it stems from scientific psychology rather than clinical medicine, because it places more emphasis on careful research, controlled experimentation, and balanced evaluation of results, behavior therapy holds great promise for disturbed and neurotic people. With ten years of solid experience behind us, I predict that in another ten years behavior therapy will have made such advances that it will be all but unrecognizable.

2

RELAX! *Treating the Symptoms of Tension*

AT FIRST BLUSH the young man's problem seemed to be medical. He was suffering—and I do mean suffering—from uncontrollable flatulence. His propensity for breaking wind at unexpected and unpropitious moments was not only embarrassing; it was ruining his life.

Ronald (not his real name) was a tall, gangling youth with sandy brown hair, quite self-conscious about his appearance. He was a student at a college in New York City and not only lived at home but took most of his meals there. As his gassy affliction grew worse, he came to classes an hour or two early, hoping the flatulence would subside before his classmates arrived. When it did not, he cut classes. When it proved unpredictable, he dropped out altogether. Riding the subway, he stood with his back to a door at the end of a car, praying he would be unnoticed. He gave up making dates.

As the situation continued to deteriorate, Ronald came to consult me. I had seen similar cases before and recognized the symptoms as stemming from localized muscle tension. Ronald was not getting along very well with his mother. He had reached the age when he wanted to leave the nest. He planned to go away to college, but his mother insisted he live at home. The very sight of his mother disturbed him emotionally, and since he always saw her at mealtime, he was constantly beset by anxiety. The resulting tension settled in his throat muscles and he swallowed great quantities of air. Once in the digestive tract, the air must always force its way out—sometimes by uncontrolled belching—and in Ronald's case it came out through the anal sphincter. Quite understandably, this had the further psychological effect of a constant fear that he would break wind, be noticed and feel humiliated. In behavior therapy the first step would be to treat the tension and later to approach the other anxieties.

The behavior therapist may treat tension directly by relaxation, and the anxiety causing it, if indicated, by one of several other techniques. Perhaps at this point we should define what we mean by anxiety. The word has many shades of meaning in psychotherapy. One popular definition —the combination of fear with the anticipation of future evil—approximates the German word *Angst*, meaning fear. A clearer definition might be the emotional state produced when a man faces a situation that is beyond his ability to handle and his behavioral equilibrium is disturbed.

Anxiety manifests itself through activity of the autonomic nervous system—those nerves that govern the muscular movements over which we have little or no control, such as the heartbeat, the contractions of the digestive system, breathing, the secretions of the ductless glands. The resulting symptoms include palpitation, constipation or diarrhea, insomnia, stomachache, and temper tantrums. However, tension also affects the central nervous system, which governs muscles we *can* control—arms, legs, torso, head, neck, face. Tense muscles are contracted muscles, and the contraction of muscles uses up energy. That is why people under tension suffer more fatigue than is normal.

To return to Ronald: Concurrent with psychotherapy I had him see a medical colleague for whatever immediate relief he could get. The physician prescribed activated charcoal tablets, which absorbed some of the source of his embarrassment. Meanwhile I began teaching him how to relax by methods detailed later in this chapter. We paid particular attention to the relaxation of his throat muscles and spent a good deal of time on this. Loud and prolonged yelling to tighten up these muscles was followed immediately by relaxation, sometimes through hypnosis. When he had achieved good muscular control here, his flatulence began to decrease and we proceeded to recondition his emotional reaction to his mother.

After fourteen sessions, Ronald's case was closed. Not only had he stopped breaking wind at the wrong time and place, but he had lost his fear of doing so. The vicious cycle which had increased his tension was broken. His throat muscles were relaxed at mealtime, even when he faced his mother. And he had gone back to college. The localized muscle tensions which had been influencing the very pattern of his life had lost their control over him.

Traditional therapists will say that Ronald's case was by no means closed, that the conflict with his mother has yet to be resolved, and that until it is, the superficial tension and its symptom of flatulence will reappear in some other form. The psychoanalyst wants to know the cause behind what he insists is an unconscious conflict, perhaps a childhood experience involving the relationship between the ego and the superego and the id. Anxiety is a danger signal, a threat, says the psychoanalyst. Determine the nature and the cause of the threat, and the anxiety will disappear.

The behavior therapist, on the other hand, says that if we can get rid of the problem, which is anxiety, we don't have to know the remote cause. If we can make the patient's life more pleasant, banish his insomnia, reduce his flatulence, or improve his disposition, we are fulfilling our purpose. The first step in trying to defuse the tension is not to probe his unconscious but to teach him to relax.

Relaxation is not so simple as it might seem. Some people have been tense for so long that they are not even aware of their tensions, although they are conscious of the symptoms—need for a drink after work, difficulty in sleeping, jumpiness, irritability.

Before beginning the relaxation, the therapist must know the extent of the patient's tenseness. Behavior therapists have devised a scale by which a patient's tension in subjective units of disturbance (SUDs) can be estimated. In the SUD scale, 0 marks complete relaxation and 100 indicates the thin edge of panic. Although the concept of muscular tension as opposed to relaxation is new to some, most patients seem able to judge their SUD percentage within a few points. One young man, whom I judged as fairly relaxed at about 30 (he was externally calm), told me he assessed himself at 80. I checked by feeling his arms, and found that his muscles were as taut as violin strings.

If the patient is unable to judge the relation of muscular tension to relaxation, I seat him with both arms on the arms of a chair. I then seize his wrist and try to wrestle his right arm away from his body while he resists with all his might. After a minute of this he is able to compare the feeling in his relatively relaxed left arm with the tension in the muscles of his right forearm, biceps, and shoulder. In this way he begins to learn to distinguish the signs of tension. I then release his right arm and instruct him to relax it. He is surprised to find it quickly becomes more relaxed than the left arm, and he can again distinguish the difference. He is learning how it feels to be relaxed.

The patient is now ready to stretch out on the couch, close his eyes, and really learn how to relax. I first ask him to picture a pleasant scene, putting in as many sensory details as possible. Some patients see themselves lying on the mossy bank of a chuckling brook in a cool, wooded glen.

Others imagine themselves lying on the beach, enjoying the warmth of the sun and sand, with the rhythm of the surf in their ears and the salty tang of the sea breeze in their nostrils.

Care must be taken, however, that the "pleasant scene" does not increase tension. One rather plump young woman, for instance, objected strenuously when I suggested the beach. "Heavens, no! Not the beach!" she said. "I look terrible in a bathing suit!"

Other patients have offered curious images as their pleasant scene of calm and quiet. One man could think of nothing more serene than lying in a tub of warm water. Another liked to picture himself lying on a bench in the locker room at his clubhouse after a strenuous session of four-wall handball, listening to male voices above the hiss of the shower, smelling cigar smoke as it mingled with the smells of sweat and liniment. The only agreeable picture one woman could conjure up was of herself sitting on the toilet seat.

For those who remember no pleasant scenes, or who could not visualize any, I have tried to create a similar effect by other means. I would tell them to picture themselves sitting relaxed in a movie theater watching the blank screen flooded with a pale blue light. Gradually a line of four blue spots appears on the screen and darkens to form letters . . . C . . . A . . . L . . . M . . . The letters gradually fade into the background again but the impression persists . . . Calm . . . Calm . . . The scene and the words "calm" and "relaxed" are all part of a conditioning process.

We are now ready for the relaxation exercises themselves. The ones I use are a simplification of a series devised by Dr. Edmund Jacobson.* Dr. Jacobson's course takes

---

* *Progressive Relaxation,* by Edmund Jacobson, M.D.

180 hours spread over six months. It focuses attention on very small groups of muscles and works on them for hours, with the same meticulous attention the Hindu yogi practices before he gains such control of his muscles that he can even stop his heart for several beats.

The relaxation series I use requires only about twenty minutes at a session and involves the muscles in larger groups. However, I use the same succession of tightening the muscles (ten seconds) and relaxing them (thirty seconds), interspersed at intervals with deep breathing, that forms the basis for the Jacobson method.

A moment ago we left our patient lying on his back with his eyes closed. His hands are at his sides, fingers open. I now tell him to curl his toes and bend his feet toward his body to tighten his foot and calf muscles. After ten seconds, I tell him to relax the same muscles, to let the tension flow out of them until the feet and legs are limp and heavy, usually about thirty seconds.

The same process follows for the thighs, buttocks, and anus; then the various muscles of the torso, followed by the neck and shoulders, the inner throat, the jaws and tongue, and finally, the more delicate muscles of the face.

I then tell the patient to picture his pleasant scene and hold it in his mind while we again relax all his muscles, this time without first tightening them. I repeat the phrase "Calm and relaxed" every five seconds or so to condition relaxation to these words.

Next I ask the patient to estimate his current SUD level. It should be down to 10 or under. If not, I try to localize the tension and work on the particular set of muscles that seems to be holding out.

Finally, since there seems to be an element of hypnosis in these exercises—at least an increased susceptibility to suggestion—I avoid an abrupt termination. I say, "I'm going to count—three, two, one. When I reach one, open your eyes. You will feel alert and refreshed."

The whole routine is tape-recorded, and the patient takes the tape home to listen to it once a day. If he does this for a week I can usually relax him so that his SUD level drops to 5 in only a few minutes. There are special abbreviated exercises for this purpose.

Readers who would like to try making a self-relaxing tape will find a complete text in the appendix.

Athletes, dancers, and others who have good muscle control are the easiest to relax. Some people are difficult to relax because they are afraid of letting go. A few patients of mine who were not used to the experience became irrationally frightened when they began to feel this unfamiliar relaxation. Some women have strong sexual feelings as relaxation deepens, and two of them actually experienced orgasm on the couch, although this is rare.

Unless relaxation is being used to counter insomnia or other sleep disturbances, the patient should not be allowed to doze off. Relaxation must be confined to the muscles so that the mind will be alert to the business at hand. Now and then I have to wake up a patient. He must be conscious for the training to be effective.

Some patients have trouble focusing the relaxation process on one set of muscles, although this is often of prime importance. One of my patients was a physician in his late thirties. Dr. B., a general practitioner who lived in the suburbs, was rather short and tended toward plumpness. His patients were scattered over a fairly wide area, which was a distinct disadvantage in view of his hangup: he was afraid of driving on bridges and open highways.

Dr. B. seemed to be a poised, easygoing, mildly intellectual person, but I had trouble relaxing him prior to attacking his phobia. He had no difficulty relaxing the long muscles of his arms and legs, but the tension around his midriff resisted all of our early efforts. We concentrated on the voluntary muscles of the diaphragm and lower abdomen, which seemed to be hopelessly knotted. We made a special tape which focused on the tense area, and he worked with it diligently at home between sessions with me.

One day he told me that he had been suffering from chronic constipation. "For ten years," he said, "I've been absorbing agar-agar and mineral oil like cereal and milk. Suddenly the condition cleared up spontaneously. I haven't mentioned it before because I was afraid it had nothing to do with relaxing my middle. But three weeks have gone by, so I guess I can talk about it now."

Relaxing his abdominal muscles had apparently led to a relaxation of the muscles of his digestive tract and to their improved functioning. His phobia yielded nicely to systematic desensitization. I haven't heard from him in some time, but as he has sent me several patients for psychotherapy, I assume he is no longer bothered by either constipation or driving across bridges.

Even when the patient is too upset to concentrate on performing the relaxation exercises, just listening to them on tape will sometimes reduce tension enough to provide significant relaxation at a second playing. On several occasions this procedure has aborted psychotic episodes. One such case was that of a young college instructor in his twenties whom we will call Mr. L. Married about a year, he was a good-looking and apparently intelligent chap but he had definite signs of acute schizophrenia. He was beset by fears without knowing what he was afraid of. He had a feeling of unreality. He lost his ability to concentrate, and had taken a leave of absence from his teaching job.

The first part of my initial interview with Mr. L. was devoted to probing his problem. It was clear that the long-term amelioration of his troubles would probably come through assertive training. However, it was my job to try to provide him with temporary interim relief. I tried a two-pronged approach. First we went through the relaxation exercises, which I taped for him to take home. I then made an appointment for him with a medical colleague, who would prescribe appropriate tranquilizers.

It should be pointed out that behavior therapy makes no claim to being able to handle the primary characteristics of schizophrenia. Therefore, the behavior therapist does not hesitate to recommend medication for the mitigation of psychotic symptoms.

There is no doubt that Mr. L. felt considerably better when he left my office with the tape in his pocket. He felt less helpless, more hopeful of being able to control his irrational fears. Things went well for several days. Then at ten o'clock one evening the phone rang.

"Bert's in one of his states again," said Mrs. L. "He's scared to death and trembling all over. He's practically cowering in a corner, whimpering."

I asked her to call her husband to the phone. I told him to turn on his tape recorder and play back our tape. He said: "I couldn't. I'm too upset to listen."

I told him to turn it on anyway, and to listen even if he couldn't do the exercises. Then he was to rewind, play it again, and do whatever exercises he could.

"Call me back in an hour," I said.

He did—and the panic was gone from his voice. He had gotten rid of his fears temporarily, and he and his wife had been helped over a rough spot.

We still had to deal with the situation that set off his panic reactions—his thoughts on the futility of existence, the insignificance of the individual, and similar depressing concepts. (He had taken a temporary job with an uncle as a stockroom clerk during his period of readjustment.) We worked out a desensitization routine which would deal with the problems that interfered with his state of relaxation, using some of the procedure described in the next chapter.

I also taught him practical tricks in instant relaxation that I use myself when unexpected blocks arise. Although I have done a great deal of teaching in my time, on occasion I am still faced with inexplicable blanks. When addressing more than a hundred first-year medical students in the auditorium of the medical college, my train of thought was suddenly derailed. I turned to the blackboard behind me, took a deep breath, held it for ten seconds, exhaled slowly while letting my muscles go limp, and turned back to face the class. My thoughts were back on the rails.

Mr. L. went back to his college, which was some distance from New York City. His problem is not solved, but it is now under control. And he is continuing to work with a behavior therapist resident on the campus.

Some people learn to relax with such difficulty that supplemental techniques must be used. The "stop-thought" technique (Chapter 6) may be useful for those who cannot control the anxious thoughts that intrude while they try to relax. For others we may try to induce relaxation through fatigue (strenuous previous physical exercise), hypnotic suggestion, or appropriate medication. The attempt is then made to condition the state of relaxation to the pleasant scene. Eventually the pleasant scene alone will sometimes elicit relaxation. Some people, however, seem incapable of achieving a state of relaxation or a feeling of calm. For them, other behavior therapy techniques have to be used.

Although relaxation exercises are used in behavior therapy most frequently as a first step in desensitization for phobias, there are at least three areas in which simple relaxation can afford relief from anxiety and tension in day-to-day situations:

1) As we saw earlier, the relaxation technique can produce sleep in situations when sleep is *not* desired. It can also be used to treat insomnia. It is true that insomnia is often caused by problems more successfully attacked by other techniques, but in 1968 a team of three therapists—Michael Kahn, then of Yale, now of the University of Texas; Bruce L. Baker of Harvard; and Jay M. Weiss of Rockefeller University—set up a test at Yale to determine how effective the relaxation training alone might be.

The therapists advertised in the campus daily newspaper for volunteers who suffered from insomnia. They got seventeen replies. "The study was based on the hypothesis that tension in large skeletal muscles is the necessary and sufficient condition for insomnia, whatever its origin," reported the experimenters.* The seventeen volunteers, of whom two were women and twelve were undergraduates, were recruited at examination time, when tensions tend to run high. However, they all had long histories of insomnia. They went through four thirty-minute relaxation group sessions over a period of two weeks. They also did three five-minute periods daily, plus ten minutes at bedtime. Of the thirteen available for posttherapy interviews, eleven reported improvement, one, no change, and one was worse because, he said, his previously reported problems had grown worse.

2) We have seen that relaxation can be effective in a case of general anxiety. It has been just as effective in relieving tensions caused by job pressures. I have previously referred to business and professional men who are so tense at the end of the day that they race to the nearest

* "Treatment of Insomnia by Relaxation Training," *Journal of Ab normal Psychology.*

bar for a drink to start the unwinding process. A number of patients have other reactions to office stresses and strains.

One patient, the sales manager for a fairly large manufacturing firm, had to make at least fifty important decisions a day involving many thousands of dollars. He was subject to enormous pressures from both in and out of the office. He was so exhausted at the end of the day that when he got home he usually fell asleep on the couch, while his before-dinner martini sat neglected on the coffee table. His wife, unhappy with her widowlike existence, sent him to consult me.

The sales manager was quick to recognize the muscular nature of his tensions, and easily learned the quick relaxation technique. Every hour on the hour during the day he took a deep breath, held it for five or ten seconds, then slowly exhaled, letting his body go limp. He found he could do this unobtrusively while reading a report or leaning back in his swivel chair, apparently deep in thought. He did it more often than once an hour if he felt himself becoming particularly tense. He also played the longer tape at home every night. As a result his daily fatigue was reduced by as much as 70 percent within a few weeks. Except for unusually difficult days, his evening nap is a thing of the past, and his relationship with his wife greatly improved.

3) The quick relaxation technique has often proved to be effective in other tension-provoking situations. Amateur public speakers cowed by a hostile audience have found the ten-second breath-holding, calm-thinking interlude a source of poise and courage. So have participants in panel discussions who are otherwise apt to be carried away by their own enthusiasm and become inarticulate. Some men with sexual problems have found the ten-second pause helpful in dispelling the tension which may arise from the fear of failure to achieve an erection (see Chapter 7).

In summary, behavior therapy attacks the problem of

controlling anxiety by dealing directly with the physical results of anxiety—tension of the skeletal muscles. There is no magic in relaxation exercises—or, for that matter, in any behavior therapy techniques. Paradoxically, learning to relax is hard work. Not everybody is capable of the concentration required. Moreover, it is not 100 percent successful. But it is successful often enough to warrant trying.

3

HOW TO COPE WITH FEAR
SUCCESSFULLY

PEOPLE CAN BE afraid without suffering from a phobia. Fear of a coiled rattlesnake is no more than common sense; fear induced by even the picture of a harmless garter snake, though, is ophidiophobia in anyone's book. A phobia, in other words, is a morbid, irrational, persistent fear. Happily, it usually responds to psychotherapy.

Psychotherapists differ as to the cause of phobias. Freudian traditionalists maintain that they stem from a conflict involving a form of sexual excitation, which is aroused in the unconscious by some person or situation of which the patient is unaware. The conflict causes an unconscious fear reaction, which is transferred to an external object. However, since the transfer conceals the connection between the original conflict and the situation that is now feared, the phobia has a specific unconscious significance symbolizing, in a distorted way, a forbidden gratification, or punishment for an unconscious impulse, or both.

The Freudians treat phobias by helping the patient himself discover the unconscious conflict and bring it into the conscious. When the conflict is resolved, the phobia disappears. The resolution achieved through psychoanalysis is a long and complex process, which may take years.

The behavior therapist approaches a phobia quite differently. To him a phobia is not a defense against an unconscious impulse or threat; it is simply a matter of inappropriate conditioning, or learning. Through either a series of minor events or one traumatic experience, certain stimuli have become associated with fear or other disturbed feelings. The behavior therapist believes that the phobia may even be purely accidental.

Behavior therapy uses several techniques to treat the phobias. Basically, the favorite methods convert the stimulus-anxiety association to a stimulus-no-anxiety association.

The usual treatment of choice is systematic desensitization, which we touched upon in the previous chapter. This method is a step-by-step process of removing the anxiety caused by the specific object or situation. In some cases this is done by using the actual fear-provoking object, but more often it is done by presenting a series of fear-provoking scenes which the patient visualizes in an ascending order of anxiety. The therapist calls this list a hierarchy.

The idea of the graduated approach to a potential or imagined danger is not a new one. Fathers have used it for ages in introducing a child to a new experience such as sea bathing. Holding his hand to give him a sense of relaxed security, the father approaches the water's edge and has the child dip one toe into the unknown. Next the child immerses both ankles. If he shows signs of fear, they retreat to shore and start over again. When the child can stand waist-deep and release his father's hand, he has a good chance of growing up without aquaphobia.

Before the desensitization process may begin, the therapist must diagnose the case accurately. In diagnostic conversation with the patient he tries to determine which specific stimuli elicit the fears so that they can build a proper hierarchy together. They list the things that frighten the patient and rank them in order from those which provoke the least anxiety to those which provoke the most.

After the hierarchy has been constructed, the next

step is to relax the patient. The relaxation must be deep and as nearly complete as possible. Unless the SUD level can be lowered to 0 or close to 0, systematic desensitization is not likely to be successful. Inability of the patient to visualize is also an obstacle to successful desensitization, although some of the less visually oriented can be trained to visualize by the presentation of objects, such as a pack of cigarettes, or magazine illustrations, before they close their eyes. The patient must also be able to sense his own feelings of anxiety, something that deeply depressed or detached patients cannot always do. In some cases, however, the galvanic skin reflex indicator may be used to measure increased tension by reflecting minute changes in skin perspiration.

With the patient relaxed on the couch, his eyes closed and his arms at his sides, we are ready to begin the process of desensitization against his phobia. The case of Mrs. J. is enlightening because she was easy to relax, the diagnosis and building of the hierarchies were simple, and the end result remarkably complete and prompt.

Mrs. J. walked up nine flights of stairs to my office when she first came to consult me, because she was afraid to take the elevator. A middle-aged woman, she had not ridden in an elevator in twelve years. Her trouble was almost certainly claustrophobia, but the sources of a claustrophobe's fear vary, and must be determined in order to construct a proper hierarchy. Her first answers indicated that she was not afraid of the elevator's falling, of being trapped between floors, or of being squeezed in an overcrowded car. She was not afraid of heights either. Hers was apparently a simple fear of being confined in a small enclosed space.

The imaginary scenes I presented to her were at first fairly remote in time and place from the immediate, fear-provoking situation. I had her picture herself at home, dressing to visit a close friend who lived on the twenty-fifth floor, too many steps to climb. Next I took her in imagination to the friend's building, across the lobby, and to the bank of elevators. At our first session she managed to push the button to call the elevator. Her SUD level at the first presentation of each scene ranged between 15 and 35. By the last presentation it had dropped to 0.

In our second session she pictured herself riding up and down in elevators of different sizes, from large freight elevators to small coffinlike boxes. Her SUD level the first time she imagined each scene was high, but at the end of the last presentation it was down to 0. When she left my office she was doubtful about using the elevator, but said she would try.

Fifteen minutes later, she was back. She said she had taken the elevator down, and had felt so proud of herself that she had ridden up and down for ten minutes and wanted to stop off and tell me about it.

The case of Jerome P. was much more difficult. Jerome, a college student at the time, had a morbid fear of urinating in his pants. His family was dominated by a strong-minded, dictatorial mother who cracked the whip over Jerome, his sister, and even his father. He remembered that the first time his problem arose was while he was coming home from school at the age of eight. A neighbor's police dog charged at him, barking. He was not afraid of dogs when I was treating him, but at the age of eight he was frightened and ran. He also wet his pants, so extensively that a schoolmate noticed it and made fun of him. At the age of fourteen he had a similar accident. He was out for a drive with his family, and he again wet his pants. He did not remember the exact cause, but he thought his mother's yelling had had something to do with it; she was usually shouting at either him or his father. At sixteen he was seized by an overwhelming need to urinate while riding the subway. He tried to contain himself until the train reached the next station, but was not completely successful. His undershorts were damp when he got off the train.

From then on, what had been an occasional worry became a phobia. There was no medical cause for his condition. His kidneys were normal. There was nothing wrong with his bladder or its sphincter. Yet he was terrified that he would urinate involuntarily at an unexpected moment, and that fear changed his whole behavior pattern over the next few years.

Since New York subway trains are unequipped with toilet facilities, the trip between home and college became a nightmare. He avoided express trains so he would be able to use the men's room at local stops in an emergency. He came late to classes, hoping that by shortening the period he would be able to hold his water until the hourly break. He stopped going to the theater unless he had an aisle seat and easy access to the plumbing. He was extremely reluctant to date a girl because he dreaded the embarrassment of having to explain why he had to go to the john half a dozen times in the course of a few hours. He even hated to stay at home evenings, because of his mother's constant and voluble nagging. He became irritable, jumpy, and difficult with his friends, who could not understand what had caused the change in Jerome.

Since Jerome had emptied his bladder just before he lay down on the couch, I had no trouble relaxing him. I began the presentation of scenes with the usual step-by-step approach, the early scenes removed in both time and locale from the scenes of greatest anxiety.

"Picture yourself at home, studying," I told him. "It is Sunday evening, and you have an early class in the morning. You will have to take the subway." I paused for a few seconds. "If you felt any tension during the scene, raise your right index finger." There was no reaction. "Now imagine that it is the next morning. You are walking to the subway station three blocks away. Make it as real as you can. You are late and must take the subway." Again I pause. "If you feel any tension during the scene, raise your left index finger."

He raised his finger, and we went through thirty seconds of the relaxation ritual. We had to repeat the walk to the subway station several times before he could imagine it without tension.

The following scenes were progressively tougher. I took him the last block to the station and down the subway steps. He imagined the stale underground smells, the rushing crowd, the roar of an express coming into the station. He waited in line to buy tokens. The rest of the session was devoted to getting him through the turnstile to the station platform, removing the tension from each part of the scene.

We spent a number of subsequent sessions getting Jerome off the subway; he put in laborious hours in the process, imagining all sorts of tortures. He had been boxed in by the crowd and had a hard time fighting his way out of the car when his urgency overtook him at an intermediate station. I had the motorman run through one, then two, local stops because the train was late—just when Jerome was told to imagine he couldn't hold it any longer. But he stuck with it.

When we found we could get through the subway sequence without unbearable tension, we dealt with another aspect of his phobia—his fear of his friends' snickers should they suspect his trouble. I had him visualize wetting his shorts slightly while talking to his professor in the presence of the class. I asked him to imagine himself at the dean's reception for the senior class, and someone saying to him: "That's the fifteenth time you've gone to the john since we've been here. What's the matter with you?"

The scenes Jerome was asked to picture were of uniform

length. So were the periods of relaxation following the first presentation of each scene, when his tension was still high. The variety of scenes to be visualized encompassed almost every aspect of his daily life. At first he was simply to picture the situations. Later he was to place himself in the same situations but to feel his bladder tension mounting. Toward the end of treatment, he could picture himself actually urinating in public.

In one of the final scenes Jerome was asked to imagine himself at a large, noisy, and fairly formal party with all his friends present. Feeling the urgency of increasing bladder pressure, he thought that, having temporarily left his girl friend with some admirers, he could head for the gentlemen's room. He didn't make it. Halfway across the room the girl friend caught his arm. "Where are you going, Jerry?" At this point I asked the patient to picture himself as unable to control the situation. He had to let go. Wetness darkened the area of his fly. Urine ran down one leg. His girl gasped, and all his friends stared. It was the height of humiliation. When Jerome could face this situation in imagination and survive, his phobia was gone.

After thirty-one sessions, Jerome was taking express trains in the subway. He accompanied a girl on a bus ride to a New Jersey resort. He went to the theater, sat in the middle of a row, and wasn't afraid to disturb others by climbing over their legs to get out. He was usually able to synchronize his physical needs with the entr'acte. He was again leading a normal life.

Jerome's case was an illustration of how small tensions can cause major disruptions in a man's life. Or a woman's. Take the case of Erika T.

Erika was a nurse in a New York hospital. She was a lovely, long-legged blonde with the blue eyes and delicate complexion of her native Sweden. She had come to the United States at the age of sixteen. A person of great charm, she was much sought after at first by the male personnel of the hospital. The interns stopped asking her for dates after she turned them all down repeatedly. When she came to see me, she said she had been living in virtual seclusion when she was not on duty.

Erika got along well with her patients, and she was competent at her job. In her contacts with her superiors, however, she was tense. She avoided unnecessary contact with both nursing and medical staffs. She did not go to the staff dining room, but ate in her own room. In fact, she spent most of her time in her room when she was not on the floor working. She left the hospital on holidays to visit an uncle, and when necessary, to do some personal shopping. When she thought she could manage it without being seen, she slipped out to go to a movie—alone.

For the past two years she had had a boy friend, a resident physician in the same hospital. She never went out with him, however, although he had asked her to dinner and the theater many times. She did allow him to visit her secretly.

When she came to see me she had just turned down a promotion for the second time, and she was not sure why. She had to begin thinking about her future—if she was to have any future. What was wrong?

It was fairly obvious that Erika was suffering from paranoid-like fears, and it wasn't long before I began to understand why. At the age of twelve, she had overheard two close friends of the family talking about her mother in terms that shocked the girl. Her mother had been fighting a losing battle with alcoholism and was then going through a difficult stage. She needed sympathetic help, not the scathing criticism of her supposed friends. Ever since then Erika had been mortally afraid of criticism. She feared people would criticize her clothes, her personality, everything about her. She was particularly terrified of eating in a restaurant, because people might comment on her European table manners. After all, American customs differed from the European, and Americans were especially critical of foreigners, in any case.

In brief, Erika had learned to associate severe anxiety with the most innocuous judgment by others or even the anticipation of criticism. She was so hypersensitive to the mere possibility of criticism that she sought to avoid any situation where there was the remotest chance of her being criticized, particularly behind her back, as had been done to her mother. The only way she could avoid this possibility was to avoid all people. So she withdrew from all social contacts.

What had to be done in terms of treatment was to get rid of her disturbed reaction to others' covert disapproval. With the anxiety gone, she would no longer need to avoid people, and her social life would begin to return to normal.

To construct a scenario for desensitizing Erika, I asked her for a list of fifteen people she knew at the hospital. We ranked them in order of their friendliness—or at least their lack of open hostility to Erika. Dr. Jones headed the roster; she rather liked him. Then came nurse Smith, dietician Brown, and so on, until we reached the lab technologist and an X-ray assistant, who teased her quite often.

Our first two sessions were devoted to teaching Erika to relax. As she had spent a good five years living with her neurosis, it was quite a job getting her SUD level down close to 0.

I began the series of disturbing visualizations by asking Erika to imagine herself sitting at a table in a restaurant, drinking coffee. She had almost finished when she noticed Dr. Jones sitting at a nearby table with a man she did not know. When the doctor saw her, he turned and said something to the stranger. His words were unintelligible, but she was to imagine from the doctor's posture that he might be saying something critical.

We repeated the scene with nurse Smith and the rest of the fifteen names on the list until Erika could picture each scene without tension. Then we went through the list again, imagined the conversations becoming more and more intelligible, until Erika could be sure she was being talked about critically. By this time she was actually eating (in her imagination), and the people were remarking on her table manners.

When she could picture this series of situations and remain relatively relaxed, we started on another one. In this series she was to picture herself leaving the hospital wearing a new dress. At the first corner she saw two people across the street who seemed to be talking about her. As we progressed she became more and more certain they were criticizing her. In the last scenes she could overhear such phrases as: "Somebody ought to tell her that she should never wear a dress like that."

It was slow and tedious going, but after a dozen sessions she began to relax. She watched television with some other nurses, and she went to the movies with her boy friend. When we had finished (it took over a year), she was eating in the hospital dining room and had accepted promotion to the post of supervisor.

What we had done was to ring the bell and give no shock—present the disturbing scene and remove any tension—over and over. We may have to present the same scene three times or ten times before the anxiety is gone and we can go on to the next scene. It is hard work for the patient and the therapist, but both of us see the gradual progress through the hierarchy and the actual changes in behavior in the real-life situation. Here lies the greatest satisfaction; it makes the work and repetition tolerable.

Another patient had to be desensitized to criticism, but

unlike Erika's case, in Richard L.'s case the criticism was real and personal. Richard L. was a young writer, a budding dramatist who had already had one play produced on Broadway. The play was unanimously panned by the drama critics of the New York press. Nobody in the world can bite more deeply and chew out more thoroughly than a newspaper critic when he gets his teeth into what he considers a poor play, and Richard was very hurt. He was a sensitive fellow who had been in analysis for two years, trying to find a solution to some personal problems. When his play closed after a few days, he was despondent. His analysis was stalled. He ran against a writer's block. He had been in the midst of writing another play, but he was afraid to put down another word. He was sure he would never be any good. He came to see me.

Richard's reaction was phobic because of the paralyzing nature of his fear. Taking the sting out of it would not mean that he would get to like criticism or that he would not be upset by it. What it did mean is that he would not be paralyzed by reading criticism, and he might even profit from it.

The desensitization of Richard had to be done on two levels. We first had to remove the crippling fear of criticism, then attack his fear of writing badly.

For the episodes with the least tension I had him listen to the reading of the least vitriolic reviews. One critic, for instance, wrote: "The central idea is a good one, but the playwright hasn't yet learned how to handle it." I then presented him with imaginary stinkers. I did not see or read the play so I had no idea whether it was as bad as the reviewers said, but for purposes of Richard's desensitization, it was worse. I had him imagine himself confronting Clive Barnes of the *New York Times* and asking the critic if he honestly thought the play was as inept as his review had said. He was to visualize Barnes holding his nose as he replied: "Ineffably atrocious. I shouldn't have wasted the space to review it at all."

The previous scenes had taken enough of the tension out so that picturing the Barnes confrontation did not increase his tension to such a degree that he could not cope with it. With each repetition of the scene, the tension came down steadily.

The second hierarchy took him through the torture of writing reams and reams of bad prose and worse dialogue. He agonized as he pictured himself writing and rewriting the same page, trying to get it right, until the floor of his study was covered with crumpled paper.

Richard did finally get rid of his block and finished his second play. It has not yet been produced, so I don't know how he will react to the reviews, good or bad. But for the time being his phobia has disappeared.

The double-hierarchy approach to Richard's phobia is not unusual in behavior therapy. Actually, four and five hierarchies are often used in dealing with a specific fear in complex cases. Another double-hierarchy case of mine was a bachelor who came to me soon after he was engaged to be married. He was torn apart by two conflicting phobias: he was afraid of marriage, but he was also afraid to tell his fiancée of his fears. The problem was: Should he or should he not go through with his commitment?

The second phobia was the simplest—a fear of anger. He was afraid of his girl's yelling at him when he announced his change of heart, and he was afraid that other people would be angry with him for backing out.

The first phobia—fear of being trapped in marriage—was actually an aspect of claustrophobia. The indecisive bachelor was very uneasy in any situation from which he could not escape any time he wanted to, although the uneasiness did not have a major impact on his life in general. He could take elevators if he had to, but often walked up several flights of stairs, rationalizing that he needed the exercise. He would take a plane if forced to go on a long trip, but he was never comfortable flying, and always drove his car when distance permitted.

This mild claustrophobia generalized to his interpersonal relationships. He would not make plans far in advance because he felt trapped by his own schedules. Marriage for him was like being caught in an elevator stuck between floors. It would rob him of his freedom of movement. What if he should meet an interesting girl and was not free to take her out? What if he didn't feel like going home for dinner on a particular night?

Systematic desensitization removed enough tension from the situation so that he could make his decision on the basis of what he wanted and not on the basis of what made him tense. He decided he would not go through with the marriage, and was satisfied with the decision.

As we have seen, Richard's fear of being trapped spread into other areas. This phenomenon is not uncommon; it is a little like the concentric ripples spreading across the water when a stone is thrown into a lake. Psychologists call this referral process "generalization." Another example of generalization was the case of Winifred S.

Winifred had several phobias—but the one that brought her to seek help was fear of men. She wanted to like men and was eager to get married, but she could not allow herself to become emotionally involved enough with any man to generate the possibility of matrimony. She was afraid that men would deliberately try to annoy and embarrass her.

This fear was a generalization of her relationship with her father, who actually did these things. She was afraid of her father because he seemed to be trying to ruin her life. When a young man came to call, for instance, Papa would make an appearance in his undershirt, two days' stubble on his unshaven face. One of our hierarchies was designed to desensitize her to her father's inconsiderate behavior.

It is easy to understand how the fear of her father could generalize to all men, but it is difficult to see how it could generalize to a fear of heights. Yet Winifred definitely suffered from acrophobia, and was terrified to go higher than the fifth floor. There was a connection between the two phobias, however, for when she was desensitized to her father's crude behavior, her fear of heights also disappeared. She discovered this when she was escorted to a cocktail party on the terrace of a penthouse and found herself leaning against the parapet, calmly looking down at the traffic in the street, twenty-one stories below.

Many cases of agoraphobia are also the result of generalization. The root cause is usually a disturbed personal relationship. Somehow the fear of being abandoned by someone close (a wife's fear that her husband will leave her, for example) sometimes seems to generalize to a fear of open spaces. Mrs. C. was such a case.

Mrs. C. was terrified of leaving her apartment. She would not even go down to the lobby unless she was accompanied by a man, preferably her husband or brother. She was afraid of dying of a heart attack, although her physician had assured her that her heart was perfectly sound. She couldn't bear the thought of dying alone among strangers to whom she was not even a statistic.

Her phobic behavior disrupted not only her own life but also that of her husband, who was very concerned about her condition. He had to arrange his business life to suit his wife's calls on his time. He often had to leave the office early to take his wife shopping. Sometimes he had to sit with her at the beauty shop while she was having her hair done. When Mrs. C. came to consult me for the first time, she was clinging to the arm of her husband. She was lost when he was not within arm's reach.

Mrs. C. turned out to be a very dependent sort of woman. Her basic fear was that she might lose her husband. Despite his apparent devotion to his wife, he was a creature of moods, and when he was angry he withdrew into himself. He would sulk for days, not speaking except to ask her to pass the butter. Her agoraphobia was generalized from her fear that Mr. C. would leave her.

Mrs. C. was given the classic therapy—deep relaxation and desensitization to the idea of her husband's moving out. She was presented with such imaginary scenes as waking up in the morning and finding nobody beside her in bed, making breakfast and eating it alone, leaving the house alone to do her shopping—in sum, actually being independent. After a number of sessions, she began to respond to treatment. As an adjunct to our in-the-office therapy, her friends and relatives were instructed to stop reinforcing her phobia by acceding to her demands for special attention.

While the systematic desensitization is the treatment of choice for phobias, half a dozen other methods have been used successfully in special cases. One based on aversion therapy is discussed in a later chapter.

Mrs. H. was an advanced case of bacteriophobia. Her fear of germs was so extreme that it would have been laughable had it not paralyzed her to such an extent that she could no longer keep house. She would not touch a plate, for fear she might infect her family with some disease she might have picked up somewhere. She wouldn't open the china cupboard or handle a cup or saucer because she was afraid she might transfer germs from the outside of the cupboard door to the chinaware. She wouldn't open the refrigerator door, for fear someone had left pathogenic microorganisms on the handle that could somehow get into the food. Faced with this impossible disruption of the household, a family council decided that Mrs. H. needed psychotherapy desperately.

A colleague of mine tried to desensitize her by imagery, but gave up after numerous sessions. Mrs. H. could not visualize. The therapist then decided to try aversion-relief treatment at the patient's home. He and an assistant attached a gadget which was in turn connected to the patient's forearm by a long cord to a galvanic device that would give her an electric shock. The jolt would be harmless, but strong enough to be distinctly unpleasant. The only way Mrs. H. could stop the current and get what the behavior therapist calls *aversive relief* was by opening the refrigerator, or the china cupboard, by touching a plate or platter, or by touching a cup or saucer.

When she did this, the current was turned off by the therapist (or, later, by a cooperating member of her family) and the disagreeable feeling of the electric shock stopped. At first Mrs. H. still recoiled from the "danger" of infection, but finally she responded to the pleasant feeling of relief when the shock was stopped. This pleasurable feeling (the stopping of the shock) became associated with the object formerly feared (the refrigerator, a plate, etc.), and countered the disturbed feeling previously aroused by the same object. To stop the shock the woman had to touch a plate or open the refrigerator or perform some anxiety-provoking act.

After literally hundreds of such aversion-relief experiences, the pleasurable feelings did begin to counter the fears and she was able to function without difficulty.

Another technique is nonsystematic desensitization, a method I have used with success for patients in certain panic states. Instead of a step-by-step hierarchy approaching the scene of greatest fear gradually, this method plunges the patient immediately into the heart of his most tense situation. It is still experimental but I have found it clinically useful.

An out-of-state colleague who heard me read a paper on this method asked me to see his sister, who had some sort of phobic neurosis and had got no relief from two years of Freudian-oriented therapy. An unhappy individual, irritable and difficult with her friends, she was apparently a chronic depressive, with panicky intervals. She could work, but had been unable to hold a job for very long. Mrs. K.'s trouble had started one weekend when her nine-year-old daughter went to spend a few days with her grandparents, the patient's father and mother. This seemingly innocent event put Mrs. K. into a mental and emotional turmoil verging on panic.

It seems that when Mrs. K. was nine years old, her father had made approaches to her that could only be construed as sexual. She had been terrified, and the memory which she thought she had succeeded in burying for years was suddenly revived in all its shocking detail. She was sick with worry that the intervening years had done nothing to mitigate her father's aberration. Would he see his little granddaughter as a sex object? Had she made a mistake in subjecting the girl to a possibly traumatic experience? The past shock, and the potential danger of that weekend, although it did not materialize, had left a wound that would not heal.

I explained to Mrs. K. what we were going to do. There would be no time-consuming deep relaxation exercises. I made sure she was relaxed, and that she was able to visualize a calm, pleasant scene. Then I said: "I want you to picture what happened when your father frightened you as a child. Make it as bad as you can—even worse than you remember it. Now don't start until I tell you. And I want you to signal me whenever you first begin to feel tension. Raise your index finger as soon as the anxiety begins."

The scenes did not run too long at first. Two or three seconds sufficed before I said, "Stop the scene. Use all your will power to put it out of your mind. Relax and picture that pleasant scene again." Allowing the initial tension to build too high is apt to harm the patient. Later, however, she was allowed to picture the worst for five, ten, and ultimately twenty seconds.

Next Mrs. K. was to visualize what might have happened to her daughter on the weekend that set off her neurosis. I asked her to imagine that the worst had happened, and to picture it in detail. Patients in this type of therapy usually are several steps ahead of me and make the scene even worse than they first described it to me.

Mrs. K. made rapid progress. By our third session, all tension was gone from her imagery of the memory and the fears for her daughter. Six months later I heard from her brother that she was again leading a normal life.

Emotional flooding, or "implosive therapy," as it is occasionally called, is a somewhat similar technique. It is a little like throwing a patient who is afraid of the water into the deep end of a pool—a sink-or-swim situation. Because of the risk entailed in aggravating the patient's phobias, some therapists hesitate to employ the flooding method, and resort to it only when no progress is made using the systematic desensitization process.

Dr. Joseph Wolpe of Temple University Medical School describes* a case in which he used the flooding method on a dentist who could not inject Novocaine because he feared the patient might die in the chair. After putting the patient under light hypnosis, Dr. Wolpe asked him to pic-

---

* *The Practice of Behavior Therapy*, by Joseph Wolpe, M.D.

ture himself giving a nerve block and seeing his patient slump forward, dead. As Dr. Wolpe describes it:

Dr. E. became profoundly disturbed, sweating, weeping, and wringing his hands. After a minute or so I terminated the scene and told him to relax. Two or three minutes later the same scene, presented again, evoked a similar but weaker reaction. The sequence was given three more times, at the last of which no further reaction was observed. Dr. E. said that he felt he had been through a wringer—exhausted, but at ease.

The difference between the "flooding" method of the Wolpe example and nonsystematic desensitization is that nonsystematic desensitization, like the systematic technique, tries to keep anxiety at a minimum and immediately counter it with relaxation. Flooding (or implosion) attempts to confront the patient with his worst fears in the expectation that the panic will wear off, as with a person thrown into the pool. Although, in the Wolpe case, the patient holds the picture only a minute or two (still much longer than the few seconds in nonsystematic desensitization), it is not unusual with this method to have the patient hold the picture for half an hour or even much longer. The panic must be given a chance to dissipate.

Some phobias respond only to what may be the most powerful of all tension-reduction techniques: desensitization in the real-life situation paralleled by desensitization through imagery. I once used the combination for a patient who was afraid of flying. Philip S. was a business executive who, although he had to travel a lot by plane, never could get used to flying. "I've been scared of flying for more than two years," he told me, "and since there is no immediate prospect of my not having to use these damned planes, I thought I'd see if there was some way of getting rid of this phobia."

First we had to find the core of Philip's phobia. Was he

afraid of being airsick? Was he an acrophobe? Did being shut up in that metal tube give him claustrophobia? Or was he terrified of being killed or crippled in a crash? It became clear that fear of a crash was his core phobia.

Philip learned to relax readily, and was presented with scenes at the airport. He saw (in imagination) the planes taking off, smelled kerosene from the departing jets, heard more flights being called over the public address system, stood in line at the boarding gate. I then had him go out to LaGuardia Airport to experience the reality. He was to stay around the airport for an hour, relaxing himself with the quick technique I had taught him to use whenever he felt the tension mounting.

Had he been anxious during this experience I would have had him repeat it several times and perhaps repeat the systematic desensitization through imagery. I had planned to follow this with further step-by-step life experiences involving longer and longer flights, but this wasn't necessary. He came through the harrowing hour unharrowed at the end. He phoned me later to report that for the first time in his life he had eaten and enjoyed a full meal in flight.

Another recently developed technique combines facing the patient with the phobic stimulus in real life and providing a guiding hand to demonstrate the harmless character of the fear-provoking object. Prominent among its practitioners are Dr. O. Hobart Mowrer of the University of Illinois and Dr. Albert Bandura of Stanford. The method, called "modeling," has been particularly successful for children afraid of dogs and adults afraid of harmless snakes.

In an example of how modeling works, phobic children are having fun at a birthday party when another small boy enters leading a dog. The tots observe from across the room while their "model" plays with his pet for a few moments. In succeeding sessions the fearless one and his pup come closer and closer to the group until some of the others get up the nerve to join in playing with the dog. Usually two out of three lose their fear of dogs after exposure in this manner.

An associate of mine at New York Medical College, Dr. Mickey Denholtz, resorted to modeling when Gerald V. came to see him. Gerald had a hand-washing compulsion. He hurried to the washroom forty or fifty times a day—displaying what is frequently a symptom of mysophobia, fear of contamination. In Gerald's case, the focus of his phobia was urine, his own or somebody's else's. Not only was he afraid that the last drop might somehow have touched his hands while he was zipping up his fly; he also feared that he might have been unaware of it and might have contaminated some other object before he washed his hands. In addition, of course, there were hundreds of objects that his fellow office workers might have contaminated with that last drop on leaving the gentlemen's room.

Gerald was asked to bring a specimen of his own urine to his second session with Dr. Denholtz. The doctor had on his desk a gallon jug of water. The first thing the therapist did was, using an eye dropper, to deposit exactly one drop of urine into the gallon of water.

Except when he lay with his eyes closed during a series of relaxation exercises, Gerald could not help staring at the gallon jug, now contaminated.

At the end of the session, Dr. Denholtz again uncapped the jug, poured a teaspoonful of the liquid into the palm of one hand, dampened the other hand and spread it well over all his fingers. This was the modeling process, to demonstrate that there were no dire consequences. He then poured a few drops into Gerald's hand and suggested he imitate the hand-washing motions.

At the next session the strength of the solution was increased to two drops of urine per gallon. Then three, four, and five drops—at each session Dr. Denholtz modeled by rubbing the solution on his own hand until all fear was drained from Gerald's contact with urine.

It should be clear from the foregoing that phobias can be successfully treated by dealing with an inappropriate emotional habit through reconditioning. The fear stimulus is broken into small segments, and each segment is associated, step by step, with some counteranxiety response. In this way the original fear reaction is dissipated and destroyed.

It must be made clear that these methods do not always work. Sometimes the inability to relax or to visualize leads to technical difficulties that cannot be overcome. More important, the fears sometimes appear to be the outgrowth of an unsatisfactory life-style, rather than inappropriate learning. The behavior therapist's techniques for modifying life-styles will be described in subsequent chapters.

4

FIRST AID: *Learning to Face*
Your Spouse, Your Friends, Your Boss

MRS. C. WAS IN trouble with her husband again. She had just subscribed to another magazine. Mrs. C. simply couldn't say no when a young salesman rang her doorbell with his story of working his way through college.

"Good grief!" said Mr. C. "Isn't there any way for you to learn sales resistance?"

There is indeed. Mrs. C. was badly in need of assertive training, one of the most effective devices in the behavior therapist's tool kit.

Many people confuse what the behavior therapist calls assertion with what the layman would call aggression. The two attitudes are quite distinct. Aggression is a hostile act or attitude, other-oriented, marked by strong elements of attack. Assertion may be defined as the ability to talk openly, directly, honestly, and appropriately about what one is thinking and feeling—particularly feeling—at a given moment. It is the assertion of one's own identity, the expression through words and behavior of the individual affirmation: This is what I think, this is what I feel, this is what I am.

Assertion is the ability to say no when you do not want to say yes; the ability to say, "No, I don't feel like going to the movies tonight," without feeling guilty about it. Assertion is also the ability to express affection, to be articulate about the tender feelings, to share intimacy with someone close to you instead of keeping your feelings to yourself.

Lack of assertion—inhibition, in other words—affects many aspects of a person's life. Often it has physical effects, producing psychosomatic symptoms such as sexual inadequacy, gastric and intestinal troubles, asthma, and headaches. Emotional patterns are also changed. Depression alternates with outbursts of temper. Spells of brooding give way to irritation and anger. Dissatisfaction with oneself and the conviction that life is futile are common with the withdrawn and painfully shy. Both the doormat syndrome and the pushed-around complex are likely targets for assertive training.

A person may find a hundred excuses for not being assertive ("I don't want to hurt him" or "It's not nice to be pushy," for instance); the real reason is that he has never learned to stand up for himself. Andrew B. was such a person.

When Andrew was my patient, I had an office in Manhattan on East 85th Street between Lexington and Third Avenues. Looking out of the window one night, I saw him drive toward a parking space on 85th near the Third Avenue corner. As he approached it, a man started to back his car halfway down the block from Lexington Avenue, blowing his horn furiously. Andrew at once drove on, leaving the parking space to the horn-blower and finding another for himself farther down the street.

This was the tip-off. I had previously been using systematic desensitization on Andrew. I now switched to assertive training. Before we began, however, I told him I had watched him give up his parking space to a man half a block away, and asked him why he had done it. He rationalized, as I knew he would. If he had taken the parking space, he said, the other man might have been angry enough to slash his tires while he was in my office.

Andrew was a graduate student in mathematics. He

was married, and working for a doctor's degree. His problem was that he was unable to complete his Ph.D. dissertation. He wrote out page after page by hand, every symbol carefully formed, every equation in copper-plate script. When he made the slightest mistake, however, he felt compelled to go back to the beginning and start over. Considering that his mathematical derivations began at about the 1 plus 1 equals 2 level, the magnitude of the revision was fairly large. He had been tearing up and rewriting his dissertation for two years when he came to see me, and he had still not finished it.

I had first tried to desensitize him to the fear of criticism, and to the fear that the work was not up to his own standards. The parking incident indicated that in fact his problem was lack of assertion. Andrew's compulsive ritual appeared to be an outgrowth of his anger and hostility at being pushed around. He had never really learned to be assertive and consequently felt (and often was) victimized by everyone. He was angry with the people who did the pushing, but he had never learned how to express his anger in an appropriate manner. So he went through life full of resentment and devoted all his energies to a series of controls that he had learned could keep his resentment in check. The discipline of his compulsive ritual was one of these controls.

Although his anger was widely distributed, most of his resentment centered on the person he lived with most closely—his wife. She was not actually a domineering person; nevertheless, he was unable to reject even her smallest request.

The first step in his therapy was to teach him to speak up to her when they disagreed. After several sessions, during which we jointly composed answers to questions that arose from common household situations, he managed to hold up his end of the discussion. He felt somewhat less antagonized, and therefore less angry. Since he had less need for his controls, his work began to progress.

When he forgot to act his new assertive self, however, the thesis suffered. One day he had been writing since lunchtime; the pages were piling up apace, and he was feeling quite proud of himself. Toward evening his wife, who was preparing dinner, called from the kitchen: "Honey, will you run down to the grocery and get me two pounds of onions? I'm completely out." Andrew promptly stopped work, went to the grocery, and brought back the onions.

A reversion set in immediately. For the next ten days he was again caught up in his old compulsive ritual. He did not do one bit of constructive work. He did keep to his working schedule, but he was merely repeating the same work he had done ten times before.

The relationship between his reversion and his lapse was clear to Andrew. He had forgotten the underlying principles of assertion. Instead of being aware of the need for honest give and take between equals, he was conscious only of the fact that onions had somehow never figured in our therapy. At his next session with me, we went over a number of things he might have said instead of going for the onions, for example, "Darling, I'm right in the middle of a terribly important part of the thesis. I can't stop now." Or "Can't you go yourself, love? I'm busy."

Andrew eventually learned that I was trying to teach him the formula: "Assertion = self-esteem." The more assertive you are, the more confidence you have in yourself, the better you will like yourself. To the behavior therapist, assertion does not mean maneuvering to get someone else to do what you want him to do. It means not letting other people push you around and communicating frankly with your peers. Assertive behavior means acting in a way you yourself respect. When you like yourself for what you do, your self-esteem goes up. Hence the formula, assertion = self-esteem.

Following this simple equation helped Andrew recapture enough of his individuality to complete his doctor's thesis successfully. It also led to a closer relationship with his wife.

Just exactly what does a behavior therapist do when a patient comes to him needing assertive training? After the first diagnostic session, I often assign him some homework: for example, reading books such as New York psychologist Andrew Salter's *Conditioned Reflex Therapy*, which may help convince the patient that if he can become an assertive person, his outlook on life—and therefore his life—will improve considerably.

The training program that is then drawn up must be custom-tailored for each individual. Creative imagination goes into all behavior therapy. In systematic desensitization the therapist must write the scenario for the anxiety-provoking scenes used in treating the patient. In assertive training he must not only provide the script, but often be actor and director as well. The program should be low-key at the outset, to make sure the patient will be able to carry out successfully the tasks assigned to him. In the beginning we pay a good deal of attention to trivia. Once the patient has mastered the trivial therapeutic tasks, he can move ahead to the more difficult ones.

Let's take the case of Dr. D., a young physician. He had been married and divorced, and was contemplating remarriage. He suffered from a mild but chronic depression. Dissatisfied with his work, Dr. D. felt that he was not giving either his patients or his career the full measure of his ability. He had stopped going to scientific meetings when his first wife became jealous of the time he devoted to them, and was neglecting research in his field as well. Colleagues at his hospital were ignoring him.

I decided that the treatment of choice should be assertive training, and that the initial program would be made up of four tasks. When I told him what the first assignment would be, he complained that he would never have the nerve to go through with it, so I desensitized him to take some of the anxiety out of approaching the situation. Dr. D. was then able to proceed on schedule with the four tasks:

1) He was to go up to a newsstand, pick up a ten-cent paper, and offer the man a five-dollar bill in payment. He was afraid of the man's probable angry reaction, but he tried it at three different newsstands. He got his change at all three, and only one man showed any annoyance. The following week, he was to try three more newsstands, paying for a ten-cent paper with a ten-dollar bill. This time two dealers told him they had no change; the third, although he grumbled about it, completed the transaction.

2) The next week Dr. D. was to enter a drug store or cigar store and ask for change for a one-dollar bill. Until he started seeing me, he had always felt compelled to buy chewing gum or a package of Lifesavers whenever he needed coins for a telephone call. He didn't have the nerve to ask for change without buying anything. A week later he was to try three more stores and repeat the request with a five-dollar bill. This time he was turned down twice, but was surprised to find that the refusals provoked little or no anxiety.

3) On the hottest days of a New York summer, when the asphalt of the street turns to putty and the sidewalks would fry an egg, Dr. D. habitually quenched his thirst with a Coke or other soft drink that he disliked. He didn't dare ask for a glass of water without being a paying customer. His next assignment, therefore, was to walk into a

luncheonette during a slack hour, ask for a glass of water, drink it, say "Thank you," and walk out again. He was delighted with the feeling of freedom the experience gave him.

4) Dr. D. was afraid of losing his temper. To prevent losing control of himself, he kept anger, like his other strong feelings, locked inside himself. So his fourth task was to telephone the Department of Sanitation, demand to speak to the Commissioner or as highly placed an official as he could reach, and complain angrily about the garbage collection in his neighborhood. As a campaign to elect a mayor of New York was then in progress, a voter had less trouble than usual in reaching top-echelon bureaucrats, and Dr. D. vented his outrage on two separate deputies. The next week he screamed at a Telephone Company supervisor about the terrible service he was getting. As he became less frightened of expressing his anger, he felt freer to speak up in other situations, too.

We were now ready to move into Dr. D.'s personal relationships and his professional life. I had asked him when we started therapy to keep a notebook in which he would record daily events at the hospital. Write down everything involving assertion, no matter how trivial, I told him, because apparently insignificant occurrences sometimes turn out to be very important.

The notebook soon confirmed the pattern of his lack of assertion. One resident in particular seemed to be deliberately delaying or ignoring his instructions. Dr. D. would ask him to take a blood specimen from the patient in 606. An hour or two later the resident had still not drawn the blood, and when asked about it, would plead that he had been too busy—whereupon Dr. D. would take the blood sample himself.

By this time my patient was aware that letting the resident take advantage of him was really not in his best interest. Together we worked out a script for the situation as it might have been played by an assertive person. We acted it out in what is called professionally "behavior rehearsal." I took the part of the resident who took his own good time to carry out the doctor's orders. When I (playing the role of the resident) started making excuses for not having set up the X rays for the new patient in 707, he answered with the lines we had written together: "Look, Doctor, I told you an hour ago I wanted an X ray on the patient in 707. I still want it, and I want it immediately. Please set it up now."

He was letter-perfect in his lines, but his manner was a little apologetic. So we changed roles. Taking the part of Dr. D., I succeeded in demonstrating that the tone and manner of delivery are just as important in asserting one's identity as the words one says. By the time the session was over he was laying down the law in a calm, firm, appropriate, and authoritative voice.

During the next week he reported two incidents in which the recalcitrant resident had seemed to be dragging his feet. Dr. D. put his lessons in firmness into practice, and the resident reacted promptly. "He's not stalling any more," the doctor said. "I think he has a little more respect for me. I know that I have more respect for myself."

As I mentioned earlier, Dr. D. was unhappy about having given up attending scientific meetings because of his first wife's jealousy. She had resented any time he gave to medicine beyond the normal nine-to-five business day. He knew no physician could keep bankers' hours and do justice to his medical career, but he was afraid that the girl he was planning to marry would be just as possessive of his time. I suggested he discuss the matter frankly with his fiancée. He agreed, but dreaded such a confrontation; he was afraid she would call off the prospective marriage.

First I desensitized him to the idea of her making a

frightful scene, and even got him to picture her giving back his ring without anxiety. We then devised a script for behavior rehearsal; I would play the part of his fiancée and he would answer the objections she might raise when he said, "I won't be able to see you next Wednesday. I'm going to a meeting of the State Medical Society to hear a paper on sudden death in sickle-cell anemia."

Another week passed before he mustered the courage to tell the girl he was going to steal an evening from her to attend an actual scientific meeting. He was surprised and relieved when she said, "I'm so glad. I was a little worried about your missing those last two meetings."

After five months Dr. D. had taken a new lease on life. He gets along better with his professional colleagues and has a renewed interest in his career. His depression has lifted. He is remarried now, and enjoys an honest, open relationship with his wife.

Whenever he feels himself slipping back into his old nonassertive role, he gives himself a refresher course in assertive training. He goes out and buys a ten-cent newspaper with a ten-dollar bill, or changes a five-dollar bill in a candy store without buying anything.

I hope that in describing Dr. D.'s therapy I did not give the idea that *how* something is said is more important than *what* is said, in teaching a person to be himself and get rid of the doormat complex. One of my patients was a typical nonassertive type, rationalizations and all. Sylvan was a giant in the office; dozens of subordinates sprang to attention when he raised his voice. But at home he was a pygmy. He had a nagging wife whom he adored. When I suggested that his feeling of deep depression might result from his failure to react to his wife's constant henpecking, he objected—as all henpecked husbands do. "I love Eileen," he said. "I wouldn't want to hurt her for the world." But he was obviously very hurt by some of his wife's remarks.

For one thing, Sylvan had an annoying physical problem. He had overactive sweat glands, and any exertion—even solving a simple arithmetic problem—caused him to perspire like a ship's stoker. Trying desperately to solve his problem, he used all the most manly antiperspirants and deodorizers. He took three or four showers a day during the summer. But the exertion of getting back into his clothes undid everything. His wife would say: "Sylvan, you still stink."

Sylvan had other problems when he came to see me, but they all seemed to stem from his lack of assertion. One day he was lying on my couch, as free from tension as he had ever been, for we had just finished the relaxation routine. "Picture yourself coming home from a party with your wife," I said. "You have been drinking quite a lot of beer. Your car is in the repair shop, and you have just walked three blocks from the end of the bus line. It is a hot night in August and you have been perspiring. You are aware of it and so is your wife. As you fumble for your keys to open the front door, your wife says: 'Sylvan, you stink!'"

Sylvan's SUD level suddenly leaped to 85.

I relaxed him again, and we repeated the scene. This time, however, I asked him to use the tag line we had worked out together when we were trying to find a proper rejoinder to his wife's disparaging remarks. When we reached the point in the visualization when he was preparing to open the door, and his wife said, "Sylvan, you stink," I had him imagine himself saying, "I know. Sexy, isn't it?"

His SUD level, which had risen alarmingly during the first part of the scene, dropped back to a calm 5 when he visualized himself talking back.

After a few more sessions Sylvan began to engage his wife in give and take; he found she wasn't at all hurt by his new self-confidence.

It may seem incredible that some people have to be

taught the simplest ABCs of being themselves in personal contacts. Another patient of mine, an unmarried woman in her early thirties, was in a constant state of mild depression. A commercial artist with a good job, she was still always vaguely unhappy. Her social life was nonexistent. She had few dates and not many girl friends. People at the office, she complained resentfully, were always picking on her. She had accumulated a full reservoir of anger backed up against the dam of her inhibited personality.

The first step in her re-education was to teach her how to handle a confrontation without apologizing for being alive. I gave her four principles:

1) You must always answer any attack. She rationalized, as was expected: "What's the point of starting an argument? It gets me nowhere." I insisted: you have to answer back.

2) You don't have to answer within a split second. Take your time, but do answer.

3) In the first sentence of your answer, do *not* use the words "I," "me," or "because." You will seem apologetic and defensive. Seventy-five percent of the time, using them is like pinning a sign on your backside reading "Kick me here." The rest of the time it is like a chip on your shoulder for an unnecessary fight.

4) If you can't think of an appropriate comeback, answer with a non sequitur. But answer.

The first lesson bore immediate fruit. The following week she reported a typical incident which she handled in what was for her an atypical manner. A sister office worker had complained loudly, "Penny, you sure left the Xerox room in an awful mess today!"

Penny's first impulse was to reply that she hadn't been near the Xerox room all week, but she remembered the third basic principle: Don't use *I* in the first sentence. So she replied instead: "You'd better apologize."

The other girl was stunned. "Apologize for what?"

"First of all, for yelling at me without justification," said Penny. "And second, because I wasn't even in the Xerox room today." The "I" and the "because" were all right in this case, for they were not used in the first sentence.

Penny had developed a backbone in a few easy lessons. Within a month her office life had changed. Her former doormat, please-step-on-me sign had been disposed of. Her colleagues stopped picking on her. She felt much better. And we were ready to work on improving the quality of her social life.

When I asked her why she didn't invite friends in, she gave two reasons. First, she didn't have many real friends; and second, she was ashamed of her apartment, which was rather shabby-looking. She couldn't afford to have it re-decorated. "Isn't there some little change you can make next week?" Well, there was an armchair that needed to be reupholstered, but that was an expensive job. It was badly torn. "Couldn't you afford to buy a slipcover?" Well, she supposed she could. . . .

The following week she managed a new table runner, and the week after, new curtains. Then, at my suggestion, she invited some people for an informal evening—a few old friends and a couple she knew only slightly. Soon her invitations were being returned. She was being included in weekend plans. She went on ski trips. She had dates. Her depression has lifted, and she has found life much more exciting.

The changes in both Dr. D. and Penny were very similar. Because they had never learned to express themselves openly, their lives were being controlled by the whims of other people—or what each thought were whims. They were passive individuals who were being pushed around like chess pieces.

By learning how to give voice to their real desires and

emotions—how to assert themselves—they began to live more actively. They could start to feel (and to exercise) a measure of control over their own fates, and by doing so, gain in self-respect and self-esteem.

Lack of assertion is one of the most common causes of marital troubles, as the case of one young couple who came to see me illustrates. After six years of marriage and one child, they were thinking of separating because they no longer enjoyed each other. Constant bickering over trifles threatened to break up their marriage permanently. Generally, an argument on the basis of an honest disagreement between husband and wife can be constructive. It can clear the air. But this couple fought over trivia, which were not only unimportant but had nothing to do with the real cause of dissension. Their trouble was that neither could say no to the other, and that since neither was a mind reader, there was no way of knowing that a yes was meaningless. Let me illustrate.

The wife was hospitalized for a few days for minor surgery. She was discharged on a Thursday morning, and her husband took the day off to bring her home, look after her, and babysit for the three-year-old. The next morning he arranged for a friend to stay with her while he went to the office for a few hours. He came home for lunch, took the child for a walk in the afternoon, and spent the evening with his wife. Saturday he also devoted to his wife, except for some shopping in the morning and an hour outdoors with the child. Saturday evening his wife was out of bed, feeling better, and watching television, so the husband said: "The Smiths are having a party tonight. Since Johnny's asleep and you're up and about again, I think I'll go over for an hour or two. Do you mind?"

His wife said of course she didn't mind—but she did. She was still feeling postoperative depression and resented the idea that her husband would be out enjoying himself with others. She was feeling sorry for herself, and her resentment carried over until next morning, by which time it was all the stronger for her having brooded about it. When her husband brought in the Sunday paper before breakfast, he dropped it, scattering the unwieldy pages all over the front hall. In trying to reassemble it, he misplaced the women's section and mistakenly carried her favorite book review with him into the bathroom.

When he emerged, his wife blew up. He was insensitive, inconsiderate, and selfish, in addition to being awkward and a total boor. He reacted, of course—but the destructive fight that ensued had nothing to do with the Sunday paper.

What would have happened if the two had been honest with one another when the real cause of dissension arose? When he said that he'd like to go to the Smiths' party for an hour or two, she would have countered with, "Honey, I wish you wouldn't. I know I'm much better, but I'm in the dumps, and I need having you around." He would probably have argued, "Look, I've been with you almost constantly since you came home from the hospital, except for three hours Friday morning. I need a breather. I'm just going for a few drinks and I'll be right back." Her final plea would have been: "I appreciate your attention and everything you've been doing, but I do wish you wouldn't go."

He might have gone to the party anyhow, and there probably would have been a fight, but it would have been a constructive fight. They would have known what they were fighting about, instead of bickering about the Sunday paper. An honest expression of their feelings would have cleared the air.

Another illustration of the lack of communication that was abrading the same marriage emerged from our therapy sessions. The husband came home one evening and announced that he would have to have a quick supper because he had to go back to the office for a few hours. He had some extra work to do and would be home late. His wife sulked. "This is the third night you've gone back to the office and left me alone. This may be your idea of a happy marriage, but it's not mine." The husband merely said, "Well, that's the way it is," gulped his martini, ate in a hurry, and left.

His wife, not having ESP, was unaware of the fact that he was under a good deal of pressure at the office. He was working on a special project, and the first draft of his report had been handed back to him as inadequate. The resulting anxiety was creating more than a little tension. When I asked him why he had not explained the situation to his wife, he seemed surprised. "She should have realized that I was worried about something," he said. Had he shared the cause of his anxiety with his wife, the whole scene would have been played on a different level.

When couples whose marriage seems headed for the rocks consult me, lack of communication, probably caused by a lack of assertion on the part of one or both, is usually the cause. Two techniques are especially useful in bridging the understanding gap.

The first is based on what behavior therapist Andrew Salter calls "feeling talk." I prepare charts which show how many times a day the patient uses phrases involving personal, "I" reactions to the day's events: "I like what you're doing" or "I don't like what you're doing"; "I agree" or "I disagree." This "track record" can be a useful tool·in therapy because a person lacking in assertion usually has trouble using the first person singular. I often emphasize this point by telling the story of a patient who insisted that he frequently used such phrases and in fact had used one just an hour before he came to see me. When I asked him what he had said, he replied, "What you're saying makes a lot of sense." I explained that while the meaning was indeed the same, the form was not, because the first-person pronoun was missing.

During the first week or two the patient usually finds that he almost never uses these phrases or, if he is self-conscious about them, overuses them. I had one patient who reported: "Doc, for the first few days my score was a big fat zero. Then I started counting the number of times a day I said 'I'm sorry' or 'Excuse me, please,' and I totaled seventy-six times. Seventy-six! No wonder I'm depressed. I go around all day apologizing for being alive."

A man's self-esteem is bound to rise when he stops being constantly apologetic in situations where he is not at fault.

When a patient gets used to saying "I like" without being self-conscious, he should begin to say "I want" or "I don't want" something. Many people find it easier to say disagreeable things about someone else than to be complimentary. One man, for example, could not say to his wife, "I like your dress," without driving his tension level up by thirty or forty SUDs; he could say "I don't like your hat" without any change.

As a patient finds these "feeling phrases" easier and easier to use, the scope of his personal reactions expands. One man who surprised himself by saying to his secretary for the first time, "I like your dress," and a few days later, "I like the way you typed this report, with all its tabular matter," soon began speaking up at business conferences. His associates seemed to have more respect for him after he said such things as, "I don't like the sound of this plan," or, "I think we'd get better results if we shipped by air." In a few months he received a significant promotion.

A wife can play an important part in helping to prepare a timid mate to ask for a raise or a promotion. A man who believes he is entitled to a raise, but is afraid of his boss, owes it to himself to ask for the increase. If there is clear-cut evidence that he doesn't deserve any more than he is getting, of course, he may be inviting dismissal instead of advancement. But if he has merely been overlooked, he should remind his boss—whether there is tension or not. The question is how to do it, and this is where the wife may play a part.

I have often engaged in behavior rehearsal with an unassertive patient who doesn't dare tell the boss he feels he is underpaid. There is no reason why his wife couldn't play the role of the boss and raise objections to all her husband's arguments. Together they could find the proper answers to counter the boss. Or if the wife fails to capture the boss's personality, they could reverse the roles, with the husband acting the devil's advocate.

The man may not win his raise, but he will certainly win his own—and probably his boss's—esteem.

The second technique I spoke of for establishing open lines of communication in troubled marriages is to have the wife express her feelings about an experience they have shared and ask her husband to say what he thinks his wife *really* means. For example, the wife says: "I don't think the Whites will be in a hurry to invite us over to their house again."

When I asked the husband what he thought his wife really meant, he replied, "She thinks White is sore at me because I had one too many to drink last night and told him he really ought to do something about keeping his dog out of our herb garden."

"Nothing of the sort," his wife said. "What I meant was that while you were out in the pantry with Irene sneaking a last drink, George White started to make passes at me, and I'm sure Irene sensed it. She's awfully jealous, you know."

In correcting her husband, she was admitting that her communication was originally inadequate.

I suggested that the couple try this method of improving communications by changing roles and trying to interpret each other's ideas when they had personal differences at home. In this way, when they disagree, they will know that they are faced with a real disagreement and not just a misunderstanding. A little assertive training of this kind may easily save an otherwise satisfactory marriage.

Lack of assertion may also affect the sexual side of marriage. I once had a patient whom I will call Pemberton, an industrial chemist in his early thirties who had finally managed to escape a domineering mother and get married. Five months later he came to consult me. His marital bliss was marred by sexual inadequacy, and he wanted to know why. He achieved occasional erections, he said, but they were rarely of sufficient rigidity to support coition. He felt confused and humiliated.

I soon learned that the new Mrs. Pemberton was cast in the same mold as her mother-in-law and that Pemberton was a henpecked husband, as his father had been. Although he felt some hostility toward his wife, he never expressed it because he felt that the right thing to do was to suffer in silence. He had been taught that the proper attitude toward women was one of awe and worship. Pemberton needed assertive treatment.

Together we prepared the scenario for a crucial confrontation. We held a number of behavior rehearsals in which he was to deliver his declaration of independence to his wife. He could no longer be a hypocrite and leave his inner feelings unexpressed, he was to say. He felt himself becoming a Caspar Milquetoast like his father, and would rather return to bachelorhood than go on in that direction.

71

When his speech was letter-perfect, I desensitized him to the tears, violent outbursts, and other reactions he might expect from his wife.

His wife was surprised and perturbed, he reported, but she had listened without interrupting him. And that night, untroubled by doubts about his virility, he had made love like a man.

Many cases of maladjustment caused by lack of assertiveness can be charged to simple ignorance. Phobias are sometimes involved in cases of withdrawn personalities and shyness, but most of them are due to lack of assertion caused by failure, for whatever reason, to learn the many social skills necessary in our complex society. Here's a specific example.

Wallace D. was a graduate of one of the better small colleges in eastern Pennsylvania. He wore his hair long, but not too long. He was a trifle overweight, slow and awkward in his movements and speech, but by no means stupid. He was a philosophy major and was considered a grind, but he had made Phi Beta Kappa. He had had no social life in his four years of high school, and during his four years of college he had gone out only once with a girl —on a double date with his roommate, who was his only friend. He did not dance.

Wallace's problem: He was leaving the country in three weeks to do graduate work at a European university, and he was terrified. He was afraid he would not even know how to stop a stranger in the street to ask directions. Could I do anything for him in the three weeks before he left? I was doubtful, but I said I would try if I could see him at least ten times. He agreed.

His knowledge of the social amenities was negligible. He didn't know how to start a conversation, but he was an eager and intelligent pupil. How should he act at his roommate's wedding? He dreaded going; the only person he would know was the groom.

I told him he had a choice. Either he could stand around like a doorpost, or he could start speaking to another guest.

"What should I say?"

At this point we went into behavioral rehearsal. I assumed the role of a second wedding guest. "Is there anything about the way I dress that interests you?" I asked him. "Do you like my tie?"

"Not particularly," he said, "but I like your tie pin."

"Then walk over and tell me so."

He did, and I told him about the person who had given it to me and related that it was made from an old French coin he had found in Europe. He asked a few nervous questions. We acted the scene again, and this time he showed much less anxiety.

When he returned from the wedding he reported that "everything happened just as we acted it." He had decided not to be a wallflower, and had approached another guest and admired his tie pin. The man had told him a story about how he had acquired it; other people had joined the conversation, and in a few minutes Wallace's anxiety was gone.

In the short time remaining before he left for Europe, I first desensitized him to the fear of accosting strangers, and then sent him out into the street to ask directions from passers-by. Next we held a crash course in the fundamentals of dating. We rehearsed asking a girl for a date. Where should he take her? What would they talk about? Would he be expected to kiss her good night after taking her home?

Wallace was a quick study. By the time he left he had had dates with two girls, one of them twice, had enjoyed them thoroughly, and felt almost no tension. In fact, a whole new life had opened up for him in those three weeks—a life he had feared because he knew nothing about it. Although I have not heard from Wallace since he left for Europe, I assume the change was more than temporary.

Assertive techniques have been useful in changing the life-styles of men far more sophisticated than Wallace. There are any number of financially or professionally successful people who are dissatisfied with the pattern of their social life, and yet, because they have never learned to be assertive, have never done anything to change it. I am thinking of people like Professor Burney, another patient of mine.

Burney was a Middle Westerner. He had blue eyes, hair like corn silk, and an intonation as flat as the Great Plains. A drama major in college, he had gone on for a Ph.D. in the same area of study. He was considered an authority in his field and had written extensively. When a full professorship in the drama department was offered to him by a well-known New York college, he had accepted and come East.

Burney, a bachelor, had an active, but not very satisfying, social life. His friends were all from the same academic background, but they did not share his interest in the theater. Burney, despite his scholarship in the field, had never been actively connected with the stage, except for student productions. Yet his great love was the living theater. He wanted to meet theater people—people who smelled of greasepaint, dined late at Sardi's, and never got up before noon. But he didn't know how to go about it. And even if he had known, he wouldn't have had the nerve. He was comfortable with Shakespeare, Sardou, and Pirandello; he felt at home with O'Neill, Maxwell Anderson, and Tennessee Williams. But he was overawed by Broadway. Could I help him?

Burney was already familiar with New York's *dramatis personae* from the other side of the footlights. He went to the theater often, usually alone, since his friends did not share his enthusiasm. He had seen several shows two or three times, and knew the individual acting styles of dozens of actors. I therefore suggested that he go to see his favorite play again, and that after the show he go backstage to congratulate the star.

"You mean just barge in cold?" he asked. "I wouldn't have the nerve."

We first ran a systematic desensitization series to remove the tension from such a confrontation. Then we worked out the dialogue for a behavior rehearsal of the backstage scene.

Encouraged by our dramatic success, the professor sallied forth to beard the lion. He was turned away at the stage door. Still, he was pleased that he had made the effort—and had even been refused—without feeling tense.

The second time he tried, he got as far as the star's dressing room, where he made the speech we had rehearsed: "I'm Dr. Burney, professor of drama at X University. I've admired your career for the past ten years, and I hope you don't mind my saying that this is your finest role." The star didn't mind, but all he said was "Thank you very much." Again Burney was pleased with his own audacity and not at all upset by the actor's cool reception.

On his fourth try he found the leading man mildly interested—enough for a ten-minute conversation and enough to make up for the next few brushoffs.

Then Burney really hit the jackpot. The star, one of Broadway's best-known actors, was very intrigued by the compliments of a professor of drama. Just what, the actor wanted to know, does a professor of drama teach a class of university students? He had never really thought about it before, he said, but now that the question had been raised, he had definite ideas about what could be taught in a classroom, and what belonged exclusively to the stage.

The exchange of ideas went on for half an hour as the actor changed his clothes. Suddenly he looked at his watch.

"Sorry I have to rush off, Dr. Burney," he said. "This has been most interesting, but I've promised to go to a party. Say, if you're free tonight, why don't you come along?"

Needless to say, Burney required no urging. A professor of drama was something of a novelty to the theatrical group at the party, so Burney found himself the center of interest for a while. He carried on several interesting conversations, made some new friends, and developed an exciting non-academic social life.

It may have been pure luck that Burney and the Broadway star found a community of interests; certainly an element of luck entered into the happy result of their meeting. But if Burney had done nothing to try to alter the pattern of his social life, nothing exciting would have happened. He made it happen, and for that he could thank the assertive techniques behavior therapy taught him.

In a totally different vein, assertive training may prove useful to many single girls in their late twenties and early thirties who are beginning to feel that life is passing them by. Not unexpectedly, they are often chronically depressed. For many, their dejection about their unmarried state spreads into other areas of their lives. A patient of mine, Lucy H., was a typical case.

Lucy, thirty, an able secretary earning good money, was unmarried and unhappy. She was not a raving beauty, but she was definitely physically attractive, and if she did not have charisma, she certainly had charm. She knew enough about men to know what she didn't want; in fact, she had refused several offers of marriage from men she did *not* want. However, she was not assertive enough to get what she *did* want.

Lucy was not a social recluse, but she felt she must be doing something wrong when at a party she met a man she liked and who was attracted to her enough to ask for her telephone number—and nothing happened. Sometimes she even stayed home at night for a week, waiting for a phone call that never came. What was the problem?

Lucy's trouble was of course her own lack of assertion, and probably that of her prospective beaux. She had been brought up to believe that being "forward" was an ungracious, unfeminine mistake. I succeeded in convincing her, however, that when two unassertive but sympathetic characters meet, nothing will happen unless one of them makes it happen. I suggested a way in which she might take the initiative without being "unladylike."

Together we wrote the script and did some behavior rehearsing. The lines were familiar until the time of party night plus three. If the anticipated phone call had not come by then, Lucy was to call the man who had been interested enough to request her number. "This is Lucy," she would say. "Are you free a week from Sunday? A friend of mine is having a picnic, and I thought you might like to join us."

Note that there is no entrapment here. She is leaving him a way out, in case second thoughts rather than unassertiveness lay behind his failure to call her. All he had to say was that he was terribly sorry but he had a previous engagement for that Sunday. On the other hand, he might say, "Sounds like a fine idea. I'd love to come!"

"In that case," I told her, "all you have to do is get in touch with some friends and plan the picnic."

The first time she tried the stratagem it worked. The man accepted eagerly, the picnic was a success, and Lucy was delighted.

I have not heard from Lucy in some time. I don't know whether she is still unmarried, but I am sure she is finding life much more enjoyable since she has stopped being inhibited.

There is nothing deceitful in nudging someone to do something he would have done himself had he been more assertive. Perhaps it is an artifice, but if it is unwelcome, it can easily be parried.

Assertive training is often more effective in group therapy than in patient-therapist dialogue. A greater variety of problems and points of view come into play, and the idea exchange in the presence of an audience can be very constructive. A group session is about half classroom instruction and half therapy. Members bring their problems to a weekly session. Causes are not investigated, but we have group discussions of situations in which an individual did not react properly in defense of his own interests. The basic theme of the course is learning how to assert oneself. Each member of the group must tell each other member at least once during the course what he likes or doesn't like about him.

Primary emphasis, however, is always on the world outside the group, since that is the real testing ground. At the end of the session, each member of the group must announce a goal for the week ahead. The goal may be to change a five-dollar bill without buying anything, to ask the boss for a raise, to announce to the wife that the seashore is out for this year's vacation, or merely to buy something mildly extravagant like a new recording of Beethoven's Ninth. The following week, group members report to each other on their successes or failures, and their fellows criticize or praise their technique.

Behavior rehearsal plays an important part in preparing for the outside tasks, as well as in correcting mistakes that cause failures. Some people who come to these group sessions are so tense about expressing their own feelings that they cannot even deal with an emotion like anger. When an individual is at a loss for words, we ask him to read a scene from a play before the group. We even furnish him with a character on whom to vent his anger. If he still fails to be convincing, one of the more assertive members of the group, or perhaps the therapist himself, models for the inhibited one until he begins to sense the relief and pleasure that comes from such assertion.

The positive results of group sessions in assertive training have been so dramatic that I am experimenting with minigroups, which combine the advantages of the group with the intimacy of private consultation. The minigroup is especially well suited for the extremely inhibited patient, who will balk at large groups; he needs the benefit of being with people who are unassertive like himself. The small group contains no more than two or three patients, plus the therapist and a registered nurse trained expressly for this purpose.

The thousands of inhibited people who have been helped to a freer, healthier, more exciting life through assertive training owe a great debt to therapist Andrew Salter. Although behavior therapy dates back to Pavlov and the 1920s, it was not until the publication of Salter's *Conditioned Reflex Therapy* in 1949 that therapists began to realize the importance of assertive techniques in reshaping personality. The therapy, in Salter's own words, "consists of getting the individual to re-educate himself to the healthy spontaneity of which his life experiences have deprived him."

Caspar Milquetoast has a chance to master his own life.

5

A CHANGE FOR THE BETTER: *How to Stick to a Diet, Get to Work on Time, and Finish What You Start*

THE DROOLING OF Pavlov's dogs at the sound of a bell introduced the conditioned-reflex principle into the psychology of learning. The stimulus-response application of the principle has produced the technique of systematic desensitization for dealing with anxieties. A given stimulus—the sight of a pretty woman or a dog or an airplane—sets off the response of anxiety. Desensitization conditions the patient to the same stimulus so that it produces a no-anxiety response.

The actions of B. F. Skinner's rats inverted this relationship and established the response-stimulus approach as a powerful concept in the psychology of learning. Skinner's formulation, based on his experiments with animals but applied with equal validity to human behavior, is defined in the following steps.

1) The animal's behavior operates on his environment. Example: The rat pushes a lever.

2) This behavior may have one of three stimulus consequences: a) Positive; for example, the rat gets food. If this takes place (positive reinforcement, or reward), the probability that the original behavior will be repeated increases. So powerful is the effect of reinforcement that one feeding will cause the animal to pull the lever fifty times before the effect is extinguished. b) Negative: The rat

gets an electric shock when it pulls the lever. Negative reinforcement leads to a *suppression* of the original response. This differs from extinction in that the response may reappear periodically following suppression. Negative reinforcement is one of the bases for the aversion methods discussed in another chapter. c) No consequences. If nothing happens when the rat pulls the lever, the probability that the original response will be repeated decreases. This is the only way extinction can be brought about. The removal of positive reinforcement is perhaps the strongest way of stopping many forms of behavior.

There is a simple way of telling whether reinforcement is positive or negative. If the original response is increased or even maintained, reinforcement is definitely positive. The reinforcement principles have led to the development of teaching machines and programmed learning.

Operant conditioning has proved particularly successful in treating children and psychotic patients, but it is effective with normal adults as well, as will be seen later in this chapter. The practice of rewarding children for good behavior has been used by parents for generations. The principle was also recognized as applying to adults by Benjamin Franklin more than a century before Skinner's rats.

When Franklin was president of the American Philosophical Society he advised the society's chaplain, "a zealous Presbyterian minister," about how to get more members to the meetings in time for prayers. As each member was given a ration of "one gill of rum" (four ounces), Franklin suggested that he would get a much greater attendance "if you deal it out just after prayers." When a record crowd showed up, Franklin remarked that the system was much more effective than "the punishment meted out by the military for tardiness or non-attendance at Divine Service."

Operant conditioning today works in a much more subtle manner, often without the subject's being aware of what is happening. The reinforcement may amount to no more than a smile or a nod of the head on the part of the therapist. For instance, should a patient, during his first interview, begin using plural nouns—dogs, automobiles, elevators, girls, headaches—and should the therapist reinforce each instance with a broad smile and an approving nod but otherwise remain expressionless, within five minutes the patient will, without being aware of it, perceptibly increase his use of plural nouns. Should the therapist then stop his reinforcing smiles and nods, in five or ten minutes the patient's use of plural nouns will unconsciously drop back to the "operant level." Reinforcement has been erased.

Operant techniques have become one of the most important influences in the psychology of learning, and probably will constitute the major area of progress in behavior therapy during the next few years. Let me illustrate how they work in a case of a psychotic patient described in an article called "The Psychiatric Nurse As a Behavioral Engineer," by Teodoro Ayllon and Jack Michael, two leading experimenters in the operant field. It is based on a doctoral thesis at the University of Houston.

Lucille was classed as a mental defective and had been hospitalized for two years. She was a constant presence at the nurses' station, where she interfered with the nurses' duties and generally harassed them. They tried to remonstrate with Lucille, and were sometimes driven to pushing her back to the ward. She persisted, however, and the nurses finally resigned themselves to putting up with her. Said one of them, "It's hard to tell her anything. She's too dumb to understand."

When behavior therapists entered the case, they decided that Lucille needed operant conditioning. What was there in the environment, they asked, that encouraged her annoying behavior? The answer seemed obvious. She was receiving reinforcement from the same nurses she was annoying. They were rewarding her invasion of their domain by giving her the very thing she sought: attention.

The therapists instructed the nurses to avoid reinforcing Lucille's exasperating behavior. Instead of paying attention to her unwelcome visits, they were to ignore her completely.

They did. During the previous two years, Lucille had averaged sixteen visits a day to the nurses' station. After seven weeks of being ignored, her visits dropped to two a day.

Therapists themselves often tend to reinforce a patient's disturbed behavior by listening sympathetically to his harrowing stories. Ayllon has described another such case, a psychotic woman he calls Helen, who had been hospitalized for three years. Helen strove for the attention of anyone available—nurses, therapists, fellow patients—by talking incessantly about her illegitimate child and the many men who pursued her with dishonorable intentions.

Some patients became so irritated by her constant talk that they took steps, some of them violent, to shut her up —thus reinforcing her disturbed behavior. Nurses also paid attention to her ravings in the hope of getting at the root of her problem, giving further reinforcement. After four months, behavior therapists moved in with their operant methods.

They spent several days listening to Helen in order to determine her operant level, and found that about 91 percent of her talk was psychotic. They instructed the nurses and the other patients to pay no attention to her ranting about the bastard child and lewd villains who still pursued her. Whenever she talked sense, they were to give her their undivided attention and approval. The nurses checked on the content of her conversation every half hour.

After two weeks of operant therapy, the psychotic content of Helen's conversation dropped from 91 to 50 percent. At the end of ten weeks, it had gone down to 25 percent. Then a strange thing happened. The irrational talk rose again to 50 percent.

Investigation by the psychotherapists showed that Helen had been "bootlegging" her hair-raising tales to persons who had not been briefed regarding the operant program. A social worker, unaware of the instructions given the nurses, was listening avidly to Helen's psychotic talk and thus reinforcing it. Several visiting volunteers dedicated to cheering up the patients had also been giving their attention—and reinforcement—to Helen. When the therapy was returned to the rails, Helen's conversation resumed its progress toward normalcy.

One of the first principles of operant conditioning is that the reinforcement must be immediate and contingent upon response. Experimental animals have demonstrated the validity of this principle; whatever the animal was doing at the time of reinforcement seemed to be the behavior that was subsequently further reinforced. For instance, chickens were given random reinforcement in the form of food pellets which were dropped every fifteen seconds. If the chicken was by chance standing on one leg when the first pellet was dropped, the frequency of its standing on one leg tended to increase. Fifteen seconds later when the second pellet was dropped, there was a good chance that the bird would again be standing on one leg, further reinforcing this behavior. It was only a matter of time before repeating the stance became standard behavior and the experimenter found himself with chickens standing on one leg, flapping one wing, and craning the neck regularly to the right.

Reinforcement can also cause changes in the involuntary body functions of experimental animals. Dr. Neal Miller of New York City's Rockefeller University has produced marked changes in blood pressure and kidney function by means of rewards. He has even succeeded in conditioning the blood flow in rats by positive reinforcement so that one ear got more blood than the other.

This work may eventually lead to operant conditioning of human bodily functions to overcome psychosomatic or even physical disorders. Experimentation in learned control of the human heart beat and blood pressure has been going on at University of Pennsylvania Medical School and the Gerontology Research Center at Baltimore, among other places. Electroencephalographic patterns—so-called brain waves—are being similarly controlled at the University of California Medical Center, San Francisco, and elsewhere, and efforts are being made to determine if epileptic seizures can be controlled through such brain-wave conditioning. The future is promising.

In the present we have already found that operant conditioning can modify the behavior of an apparently hopeless schizophrenic. Again we are indebted to Dr. Teodoro Ayllon for describing the experiment which he carried out with Eric Haughton.

For their demonstration the therapists selected a fifty-four-year-old woman, a withdrawn schizophrenic who had been hospitalized for twenty-three years. During nearly a quarter of a century her life had consisted of lying in bed in the ward or on a couch, smoking. She had refused all activity and took no part in recreational affairs.

The therapists arbitrarily selected the behavior they wanted the patient to adopt. Since she spent most of her hospital life in a reclining position, they decided to impose on her an erect stance; for no reason except that it seemed foreign to her daily behavior, she was also to be holding a broom. As she was an inveterate smoker, cigarettes were to be the reinforcement. To get the broom into the picture, the therapists used the operant technique known as "shaping."

Shaping consists of leading the patient step by step in the direction of the desired behavior by a combination of suggestions and reinforcements. When the desired behavior is not in his current behavioral repertory, it obviously cannot be reinforced. In that case the therapist takes some variation of the current behavior that seems to point in the chosen direction and reinforces it. By reinforcing the variations, the patient's behavior is gradually "shaped" until it takes the desired form and eventually becomes part of his regular pattern.

A staff member approached the patient's bed holding the broom upright. When the patient accepted the broom herself, another staff member gave her a cigarette. The details of the experiment—the various sizes of cigarette used for specific purposes, for example—are unimportant to this account. Suffice it to say that within a few days the patient spent most of her waking hours pacing the ward with her broom. She resisted all efforts by staff members or other patients to take the broom away from her.

In this case the patient was deliberately taught to behave in a bizarre manner. This raises the important question of whether or not much of the peculiar behavior shown by hospitalized patients may have been inadvertently taught them by hospital staffs. Can we really differentiate between bizarre behavior that has been learned and that which is part of the patient's condition? To test this point, two psychiatrists were invited to watch the patient from behind a one-way mirror and to evaluate her behavior.

Their conclusions, arrived at independently, may be summarized as follows:

To Dr. A., "The broom represents for this patient some essential perceptual element in her field of consciousness. On Freudian grounds it could be interpreted symbolically. On behavioral grounds it could perhaps be interpreted as a habit which has become essential to her peace of mind." Dr. A. saw her performance as "stereotyped behavior common to regressed schizophrenics" and rather analogous to the behavior of small children who are possessive about their favorite toy.

To Dr. B., the "constant and compulsive pacing while holding a broom could be seen as a ritualistic procedure, a magical action . . ." arising from "deep-seated unfulfilled desires and instinctual impulses." Dr. B. thought the patient might be considering the broom in one of three ways: 1) as a child who gives her love and to whom she in turn gives devotion; 2) as a phallic symbol; 3) as the scepter of an omnipotent queen.

Here is a clear answer to our question. Two learned men interpreted a case of simply conditioned behavior in complex terms involving the patient's state. At present, behavior therapists believe that most disturbed patterns of hospitalized patients are the result of learning within the hospital situation.

To change what is learned by the patient within the hospital, the concept of "token economies" is sometimes introduced. Although reinforcement is generally a much simpler process in hospitals, where it can be applied under carefully supervised conditions, it is not always possible to follow patients around to give the reward at the exact moment of the desired behavior modification. To meet this situation, a system of secondary reinforcement by tokens, or rewards, has been instituted at a number of hospitals—by Ayllon at Alma State in Michigan, for instance; by Schaefer at Patton State in California; by Krasner, Haughton et al. in a dozen other hospitals. At these institutions, staff members are trained to give out tokens when they see a patient performing in a desirable manner. For example, a bedridden patient is given a token when an orderly sees him sitting on the edge of the bed. Later he gets a token when he stands up, and still later, when he ventures as far as the day room.

The patient can use these tokens for his reward, which must be custom-tailored for each individual. The tokens may be used for permission to take a walk on the hospital grounds, to watch television, or to attend social functions. A certain number of tokens may be required to have lunch in the dining room. It has been noted that when a token program is discontinued, patients regress. The system has been found to work with all types of patients, regardless of diagnosis or age.

The Veterans Administration Hospital at Palo Alto, California, has established a token ward which has an atmosphere totally different from the dreary hopelessness that so often marks the wards in public hospitals peopled by chronic cases. Not only are the patients more adaptable, but there is a different attitude among the staff. Nurses, orderlies, and other aides consider it a matter of prestige to work in the token ward and take part in the reinforcement program.

Token economies can become highly mechanized. At the Patton State Hospital in California, Dr. Helmuth Schaefer is already experimenting with an automated ward. Television cameras are everywhere—in the bedrooms, the day room, the corridors. A technician sits in a central control room monitoring a bank of closed-circuit screens. When he sees a patient doing something favorable, he punches coded signals onto a tape, which is fed into a computer. The computer has been programmed to note which behavior is to be reinforced for each patient and automatically dispenses tokens.

Suppose John, a withdrawn case, says "Hello" to a fellow patient. Watching on a television screen, the technician punches the tape and feeds the computer. If this type of social interaction has been scheduled as reinforcement for John, a loudspeaker near him says, "Good, John, you earn three tokens," and the tokens drop into a nearby receptacle. These tokens are eventually exchanged for bed, meals (everything must be earned) or special privileges.

This work is still being evaluated, but the preliminary findings are most encouraging.

Even when a schizophrenic is not completely cured, the transition from the ward to life in an open society is made more possible. Dr. John Henderson has founded a halfway house in Philadelphia which operates on a token economy and is meant to ease still further the transition from hospital to home.

And Dr. Francis Cheek of Princeton, aware of the growing number of American families with schizophrenics in their midst, is pioneering the introduction of operant procedures in the home and instructing the patient's family in the use of operant methods.

In fact, the spread of operant therapy in more and more hospitals marks the first time that purely behavioral methods, without auxiliary drug therapy, have been successfully used in dealing with schizophrenics and retarded development cases.

Other institutions have also been undergoing examination for the past few years. Similar conditions exist in many schools. We have seen that much of the withdrawn, uncontrolled, and bizarre behavior of long-hospitalized, backward patients has actually been learned by them as a result of reinforcement, however inadvertent, within the hospital itself. In somewhat the same way, reinforcement contingencies in certain classrooms actually encourage disruptive or inattentive behavior by pupils. Behavior therapists have had some success in training teachers to cope with such situations systematically and successfully. (This development is discussed further in Chapter 9.) Relatively nontechnical manuals to acquaint teachers with operant methods are now available.

Corrective schools for young delinquents are also being studied with similar findings. Research is going on that may result in changes in the structure of these institutions based on operant principles. Prisons, homes for the aged, training centers for the handicapped, and similar institutions are coming under increasing scrutiny. There has even been some preliminary work in the area of applying operant principles to the hard-core unemployed. Finally, it must be noted that operant methods have already produced major changes in the training and treatment of the mentally retarded.

But what about the nonhospitalized patient? What do we do when the patient is not psychotic, but is a normally neurotic character with a minor problem in behavior? Suppose the problem is a matter of getting to work on time—a common complaint—and the behavior therapist sees the man only once or twice a week. How can the therapist reinforce the patient's behavior if the therapist is not in the office to see that he gets to his desk promptly at nine o'clock, instead of his usual ten or fifteen after?

First we determine what the reward is to be. The man may dote on rich desserts for lunch, or an ice-cold martini or two before dinner. Neither a whipped-cream parfait nor a chilled cocktail seems appropriate at nine in the morning, the time the reward should be given if reinforcement is to be immediate. The patient is asked to keep an accurate record of his punctuality on a chart marked off according to days of the week. I ask him to check off the days on which he beats the clock. He agrees to show me his chart every time he comes for consultation. He must show two consecutive red checks—perhaps three or four as the program advances—to earn his daily martini during the following week.

The success of this method depends on the motivation of the patient. If his job is in jeopardy because of his chronic tardiness, his response is apt to be positive. If lack of punctuality means merely that he may be passed over when promotions are due, he may cheat and have his martini regardless of what time he gets to his desk.

If positive reinforcement does not work, I try negative reinforcement; that is, I introduce some element of punishment. Before we start the program, we make a list of the organizations that the patient really hates: the Ku Klux Klan, the American Nazi Party, or the Black Panthers, for instance. I then have the patient write checks for twenty or twenty-five dollars to one or two of them. I also ask him to write covering letters explaining that his contribution is to encourage them to keep up the good work. He addresses the sealed envelopes and leaves them with me. When the patient fails to make a nine o'clock entrance even once during the week, I mail one of the letters.

The patient's negative reinforcement becomes increasingly negative when he starts getting thank-you letters and hate literature from the organizations on his blacklist. The least motivated characters often give up at this point. Some try to stop payment on their checks. Others stop the treatment.

A problem that is as common as tardiness, and that also can be treated by operant methods, is the inability to study. Many college students come to the behavior therapist with the complaint that they simply can't get down to studying.

The reinforcement for acquiring better study habits must of course be tailored to each individual. The reward for one young man who lived with his family while attending college in New York City was the use of the family car on Saturday night. In this case, too, the patient had to keep a chart, checking off his accomplishments day by day and bringing them to me before Saturday night to determine whether he was entitled to his reward.

The task assigned to this lad who couldn't study was quite simple. He merely had to sit at his desk from Z o'clock to Z plus Y, with an open book before him. For the first few days the study period was only ten minutes, but it had to be strictly observed. Then it was lengthened to twenty minutes; next to half an hour. After a few weeks he was locked up with his book for an hour and a half, still trying to earn a Saturday night with the family car.

The reward for another patient of mine was a date with a girl who was cooperating with me.

Whatever the reinforcement—football tickets, an introduction to an opera star in her dressing room, or a European vacation—it will not work unless the student is really motivated.

One new approach to positive reinforcement, called *covert reinforcement*, has recently been introduced into behavior therapy. By this method, the reward is meted out on the plane of fantasy. Covert reinforcement has been pioneered by Dr. Joseph R. Cautela of Boston College, the man who also introduced covert sensitization, described in the chapter on aversive therapy. Dr. Cautela's method consists in presenting to the patient both the desired behavior change and the reinforcement in imagery. To illustrate, let me describe the case of Morgan B.

Morgan was a brilliant Wall Street analyst in his mid-forties. He had a master's degree in business administration and a Ph.D. in economics. His job was to investigate the corporate plans, new products, economic structure, and production facilities of firms whose stock was on the market, and to report on the soundness of an investment in the enterprise.

Morgan's judgment was highly regarded in the Street. His ability to probe beneath the surface and come up with an accurate assessment won him high praise. His oral reports were a delight to his employers. He had inordinate trouble, however, with his written reports. Because he simply could not get down to the actual writing, he had already lost two jobs and was on the verge, he thought, of losing his third.

He had made serious efforts at overcoming his problem. He had spent several years in analytically oriented therapy. He had tried hypnosis. Nothing had helped. When he came to me I decided to try covert reinforcement.

I first broke down the report-writing process into short steps: arriving at the office, sitting down and clearing the desk, taking the appropriate file from a drawer, reading his notes, making a brief outline, writing a first draft, rewriting and editing the final draft. Next we had to find positive reinforcement. What can you think of, I asked him, that would give you the greatest immediate pleasure? Since he was a man who loved music, Morgan had no trouble finding an answer. He loved Bach's *Art of the Fugue*. He would close his eyes and enjoy listening to it in his imagination.

Next we went through the routine of report-writing step by step in imagination. Morgan closed his eyes and was instructed to signal me when he had visualized each step. I would then say, "Reinforce," and he was to listen mentally to the Bach. After about fifteen seconds of his fantasy music, I would ask him to picture the next step in his writing. He signaled me when his visualization was complete and I would again call "reinforce." Morgan again listened to Bach with his mind's ear for a quarter of a minute.

I taped the routine the second time around, and

Morgan took the tape home to play five times before going to sleep. He also played it twice before going to his office the next morning. Once at his desk he followed the routine faithfully, enjoying his phantom Bach at the intervals between the steps of writing his report.

He successfully conquered the block against putting words on paper, but unfortunately this did not provide a permanent solution to his problems. His employers, seeking to make even fuller use of his talents, assigned him new and different tasks. Adjusting to them called for work in assertive training, which he is now getting.

We saw in a previous chapter that assertive therapy has on occasion been able to rescue a tottering marriage. It has been my experience that operant methods can be used for the same purpose.

In a successful marriage husband and wife tend to give each other positive reinforcement for behavior pleasing to them. For example, the husband unexpectedly brings home a bunch of roses for his wife. The wife is surprised and delighted and shows it both in words and actions. She reinforces the thoughtful gesture by embracing him, kissing him as soundly as if he'd been away for a week, and talking about the flowers as she arranges them in a vase. Her reinforcement of this affectionate gesture is bound to ensure its repetition by the husband.

Positive reinforcement is a two-way street. If buttermilk biscuits or homemade corn bread appear on the breakfast table, instead of the usual presliced production-line toast, and the husband puts down the *New York Times* and says, "Darling, these are the best biscuits you've made in ten years," he is likely to get his favorite breakfast next Sunday. Otherwise he may have to share his wife's Metrecal.

But if there is no positive reinforcement—even without negative reinforcement—the gesture is wasted on both partners. For example, let's say the husband brings home flowers as before. The wife accepts them without a word and puts them on the coffee table as she says: "I wish you'd speak to George Smith tonight. The Smith kids were riding their bicycles over our lawn again this afternoon. I complained to Mrs. Smith but she says they did it only because our Laura dared them. After all the money we spent to have it reseeded. . . ." And while hubby is out in the pantry making himself a double manhattan, she picks up the flowers and sticks them in a bowl. The husband has received no positive reinforcement; chances are the bringing-flowers-home gesture will be extinguished.

Or the husband ignores the tempting aroma of the freshly baked biscuits and remains hidden behind his *Wall Street Journal*. When his wife asks, "Don't you want a biscuit this morning, darling?" he merely grunts and gropes around the edge of his newspaper—hardly a gesture to increase the frequency of the biscuit-making behavior.

In a bad marriage one or both of the partners gives the other a peculiar kind of reinforcement. For example, the husband brings home flowers, but he has an ulterior motive: he is trying to escape the punishing treatment he is getting from his wife. She has been sulking for two days because he lost his temper over her overdraft at the bank, and he wants to make peace. When he hands her the flowers, she says, "What do you feel guilty about now? Let me smell your breath."

Neither the aversion treatment by the wife, the attempt at aversion escape by the husband, nor the negative response by the wife is particularly conducive to marital understanding. When one partner tries aversive treatment on the other, he or she is likely to respond in kind and the vicious circle begins. When peace offerings are scorned, the goal of the marriage becomes avoiding aversion rather than sharing positive feelings.

The idea of positive social reinforcement—a reward, even if it is only a smile, for desired behavior—is quite simple. But the desired behavior change must be defined very clearly. It is not specific enough for the wife to tell the therapist that she wishes her husband were a little more loving. She must describe the particular direction which she would like his behavior to take. For example, he should kiss her when he comes home at night, notice the new dress she is wearing, show some interest in her daily activities, remember birthdays and odd anniversaries, bring candy or flowers occasionally. Then the therapist has something to work toward.

This chapter has deliberately simplified the techniques of operant conditioning. Although, as in other aspects of behavior therapy, a great deal of highly technical material must be considered in devising an operant program, the basics *are* simple.

To encourage desired behavior, three steps are involved: 1) The behavior to be changed must be clearly defined. Either the husband brings home flowers or he does not; either the wife hugs him or she does not. 2) The reinforcement must be predetermined. It may be a loving word from the spouse, a ticket to a football game, or an olive in the martini. 3) The reinforcement must be made contingent on the behavior. The hug from the wife is contingent on the husband's bringing home flowers. No flowers, no hug; flowers, hug.

To stop unwanted behavior, the first step is again to define the exact behavior clearly. The next step is to try to discover which consequences of the undesired behavior are serving to reinforce it. Very often this may be the attention aroused by the unwanted conduct, even if the type of attention shown seems unpleasant at first glance. The unruly pupil may seem to cringe under the angry teacher's scolding, but the scolding is definitely a kind of reinforcement. The third step is to stop reinforcement.

Two points of caution must be observed in withholding reinforcement. When reinforcement is withdrawn, the withdrawal must be total. Stopping reinforcement on four occasions but giving it on the fifth puts the behavior to be modified on what is called an "intermittent reinforcement schedule," which makes extinction more difficult. Second, a very common first reaction to withdrawal of reinforcement is an *increase* in the behavior to be extinguished. However, if reinforcement continues to be withheld, the frequency of that behavior will eventually diminish.

How can anyone know if he is on the right track with his operant program? I can only repeat what I have said before: If it works, it is the right therapy.

6

BREAKING THE HABIT: *How to Stop Gambling, Drinking, and Other Odd Habits*

AVERSIVE THERAPY, an important instrument in the behavior therapist's tool kit, was widely used long before behavior therapy became a recognized discipline. Old-fashioned parents did not spare the rod on the potentially spoiled child. Early association of undesired behavior with pain or other disagreeable experience was designed to turn a premature juvenile delinquent into a socially acceptable citizen. The same principle applies to adults given to excesses or unwanted habits.

Sometimes people learn what the psychologist calls "maladaptive behavior patterns," such as uncontrolled smoking or drinking, fetishism, homosexuality, transvestism, or compulsive gambling. If one of these patterns begins to interfere with some aspect of a person's life, he may want to get rid of it. Many who do are able to accomplish the change by themselves. Others seek help.

The aversion techniques are most often employed by behavior therapists to remove undesired habits. They have been quite successful with some habits such as fetishism. With others—alcoholism, smoking, and drug addiction—the results are inconclusive at present, although prospects for the immediate future are encouraging.

Aversion treatment aims to remove the undesired habit by connecting it with a decidedly unpleasant emotional tone, usually in one of two ways. The first is basically the

Pavlovian method of pairing stimuli. As we have seen, in systematic desensitization we pair an anxiety-provoking stimulus (such as being rejected) with a counteranxiety stimulus (such as the feeling of no tension). Aversion therapy pairs the characteristics of the undesired behavior with a painful stimulus, so that the unwanted practices become associated with pain and are inhibited.

The second model of aversion is based on Skinnerian, or operant, methods, described in the previous chapter. In that chapter we found that when a certain type of behavior is followed immediately by negative reinforcement (punishment), the response tends to be suppressed. Suppression is particularly useful when the reinforcement that maintains the habit cannot be defined or controlled.

Many forms of aversion are available, but because precise timing is important, a painful but harmless electric shock administered in conjunction with some aspect of the undesired behavior has proved most effective. The electrodes are usually attached to the patient's forearm or fingers, or occasionally to the leg. The current is often of fairly high voltage but of fractional amperage so that it may be painful without causing burns.

The shock method has produced some dramatic results in the field of sexual aberrations, particularly fetishism and transvestism. Other techniques of behavior therapy, such as assertive training and systematic desensitization, have been used in conjunction with aversion in these cases, but the electric shock treatment deserves most of the credit. Let us consider the case of Victor M.

Victor, a quiet, shy, balding man of thirty-one, was a high school teacher, and had been married for three years. There were no children. He had had no sexual experience prior to his marriage.

His trouble began when he saw the motion picture *Gone with the Wind*. He was so stimulated by the film that he began having sexual fantasies; he pictured himself as Scarlett O'Hara, surrounded by a bevy of hoopskirted beauties. He visited a theatrical costumer and purchased an ensemble of the Civil War period—hoop skirts, bodices, lace-ruffled pantalets and all.

His wife was somewhat surprised when he started walking around the house in 1860s women's fashions. When he made love to her by elevating the hoopskirt to a convenient angle, she was thunderstruck. And when the practice of sexual intercourse in period costume seemed to be settling into a permanent pattern, she raised her voice in strident protest.

Victor tried to meet his wife's objections, but it was beyond him. He could not give up his hoop skirts. Undressing for bed, he could not control the automatic impulse to put on some part of his costume. So he came to me for help.

The usual procedure in cases like Victor's is to try to establish an alternative pattern of behavior before starting aversive treatment. We desensitized Victor to having intercourse with his wife while he was completely nude. The tension soon disappeared from the sex scenes presented, but the automatic transvestism continued in the bedroom. Aversive techniques were called for.

Victor was instructed to bring his Scarlett O'Hara costume to the next session, at which he was to be wired to receive electric shocks. He was stripped to the buff, and the electrodes were attached to his legs with a long cord that would not impede his mobility. When he reached for the ruffled pantalets he got his first electric shock. Since it was unexpected, it startled him; the painful sensation continued until he dropped the garment. He picked it up again and continued with his costuming.

The punitive shocks also continued sporadically. Victor never knew when the next one was coming. He continued to put on his hoop skirt, adjust his bodice, and walk around my office just as he had done at home. At irregular intervals he winced when the current was turned on.

After a week of daily treatments, he lost his enthusiasm for the Scarlett O'Hara costume, but he continued to put it on faithfully despite his anticipation of the painful shock he knew was coming sometime during the masquerade. After four weeks, his wife reported he had achieved successful coitus—without hoop skirts.

Some months later he was on the verge of a relapse. However, he came in for a few booster shocks, and the fantasies disappeared. Two and a half years after his first treatment, Victor reported that he was still safely anchored in the twentieth century, and that he was continuing to enjoy sexual relations with his wife in the altogether.

Perhaps the most rapid and dramatic elimination of a sexual problem by aversion therapy was accomplished by the resident psychiatrist at New York Medical College Hospital. The subject was an automobile mechanic with a diaper fetish. He was a married man with two children, able to function well sexually, but at odd times he engaged in bizarre supplementary acts. He sometimes took one of the baby's diapers, folded it in a certain way, and pinned it about his groin. Then he masturbated until he ejaculated into the diaper.

He followed this ritual seven or eight times a week, and it interfered with the frequency and success of his marital performance. His wife knew about his peculiar habit and worried about it. She was finally able to persuade him to come for help.

The resident interviewed the mechanic to learn the details of his ritual. He then reproduced the setting down to the exact fold of the diaper, and scheduled the first session. When the patient reached for the folded diaper he received a stiff electric shock to the forearm. During the next three minutes he touched the diaper ten times and was painfully shocked each time.

The aversive treatment continued for two weeks—ten working days, three minutes at each session, for a total of thirty minutes of aversion therapy, exclusive of the initial interview.

The mechanic never came back. A follow-up check after nine months disclosed that he was still rid of his diaper fetish and that his marital relations had improved markedly.

A much more complicated case of fetishism, one which had serious consequences for the patient, was reported by Dr. Malcolm Kushner of Miami, Florida. His patient was an ex-Marine with a panty fetish.

Jack L., who was thirty-three when he was sent to Dr. Kushner for therapy, had begun stealing women's panties from clotheslines at the age of twelve. He put on the panties and masturbated. He was excited by illustrations of feminine underwear in magazine advertisements, and lingerie displays in shop windows.

As he grew to young adulthood, he attempted sexual intercourse but found himself impotent. To compensate for his lack of virility, he learned to box, took courses in body building, and joined the Marine Corps. He was still incapable of intercourse with women, however, and he still masturbated secretly while wearing panties.

When he left the Marines he joined a tough neighborhood gang and became an active street brawler. He was arrested for assaulting a police officer, convicted, and sentenced to twenty-one months in a reformatory. He served his term and was discharged—still a fetishist.

Then he broke into a hotel room, looking for women's underwear, stole some luggage to carry it away in, was caught and convicted. This time he was sentenced to six years in prison. The correctional establishment directed that he be sent for psychotherapy.

Dr. Kushner wired him for shock treatment by means of two finger electrodes. Four to six different stimuli were presented to the patient, some actual objects, some pictorial representations, others imaginary concepts. Sometimes nylon panties were placed in his hands, occasionally he was shown an illustration from a magazine advertisement showing a shoulder-to-knees view of a woman from the rear, at other times he was asked to imagine a window display of lingerie, or a clothesline bright with flapping panties. At each presentation he was given a painful shock. One minute was allowed to elapse between each shock and the next stimulus. Every session lasted from twenty to thirty minutes, and he came for therapy three times a week.

After fourteen weeks the fetish had lost its power to stimulate, and therapy was discontinued. A month later, however, the patient suffered the slight relapse which he had been warned to expect. He found himself stopping in front of a shop window to stare at a display of lingerie. He came in promptly for two booster sessions, and has had no subsequent trouble.

Toward the end of the aversion treatment, the ex-Marine was given a concomitant course of systematic desensitization for his sexual impotence. Eighteen months later he reported that he was still free of his fetishism, had married, and was enjoying normal intercourse.

The three cases we have discussed have more than passing interest in psychotherapy because fetishism and transvestism are very difficult to treat by traditional methods. One survey finds only four cures of fetishism reported in the entire body of psychoanalytic literature, while an increasing number of cures are being reported in the literature of behavior therapy. More and more the aversive methods appear to be the treatment of choice for these conditions.

Shock treatment has also produced favorable results in treating homosexuality.

Three stages are involved in dealing with male homosexuals through behavior therapy. First, we must establish an alternative form of behavior. If his preference for males arises in part from his fear of women, we must remove the tension caused by this fear. This can be done by systematic desensitization or by assertive training. Second, we must associate pleasant sex feelings in the patient with the female presence. For instance, he must be encouraged to masturbate, not necessarily to the point of ejaculation, while looking at sexually exciting pictures of nude women. The third stage is the aversion treatment per se. The patient is given the electric shock while looking at slides that correspond to his homosexual fantasies.

The technique works as follows. Some therapists instruct the patient to buy physical-culture magazines containing nude pictures of body builders and other attractive men. In this way, they contend, he is sure to get the kind of stimulus that will arouse him. I prefer to have the patient look through my extensive library of slides of men and women, and rank them in the order in which they appeal to him, from 0 to 3. Then we arrange them alternately in a carrousel tray, beginning with a low-ranking male followed by a high-ranking female. The patient holds the slide-changer control in one hand; electrodes which I control are attached to the other.

The patient is instructed to look at the picture of the man as long as he has any feeling of pleasure. When this feeling stops, he can push the button on the slide changer and the next slide appears. If he is still looking at the picture after eight seconds, he receives a strong shock and he then changes the slide. The patient can avoid the shock by changing the slide before eight seconds are up; he usually does about two thirds of the time.

The next slide shows a lovely woman. No possibility of shock is associated with this picture. The method of alternating slides connects unpleasant associations with the male (homosexual) stimulus, and pleasant overtones with the female (heterosexual) stimulus. In all, twenty to thirty pairs of slides are shown to the patient in brief daily sessions for periods ranging from three weeks to two months.

The two English psychotherapists who developed this technique, Drs. M. P. Feldman and M. J. MacCulloch, have reported a high rate of cure in a few weeks. Two-year follow-up studies have shown that very few patients tend to revert to homosexuality.

A variation of this technique has been found effective in controlling the homosexual fantasies of a basically heterosexual male. The case of Arthur J., a patient of mine, illustrates this procedure.

Arthur, a man in his middle twenties, made a good living as a waiter. He had many acquaintances, and on the surface lived the good life. At the time he consulted me he was living with a young woman with whom he had occasional sexual intercourse—without difficulty but also without satisfaction. Arthur was constantly plagued by homosexual fantasies. Even during sexual intercourse he could arouse himself only by thinking of nude men. He had had no homosexual experiences, however, and did not want any.

The first step in treating Arthur was to assume that he had some fear of women. Systematic desensitization to women in general and to heterosexual intercourse in particular was tried, without success.

Arthur was also told that while engaging in either coitus

or masturbation, just before ejaculation—at the moment he usually pictured nude men—he was to deliberately switch his fantasy to a nude woman. In this way his sexual excitement might become associated with the female.

When it became apparent that systematic desensitization was ineffective, we moved to stop the homosexual fantasies directly by using slides. We did not specially select the slides, but projected a paired series used by another patient. The aversive shocks were given when Arthur lingered over the pictures of males.

In addition, Arthur was given a hand shocker to take home. Ten times each evening he was to start making up a homosexual fantasy. When the image began to take shape, he was to give himself a shock. After the tenth shock, he was to put the apparatus away, relax, and dream up a heterosexual fantasy.

At the end of a week, Arthur reported a decrease in his homosexual fantasies of about 15 percent, but no transfer to spontaneous heterosexual ones. The change suggested we were on the right track, however, so we continued aversive treatment.

During the next few weeks we also added assertive training to improve his ability to speak openly to women. Soon heterosexual fantasies began to appear spontaneously, and there was a marked decrease in his homosexual thoughts. He was able to engage in coition without thinking of nude men. He was getting much more enjoyment from sex, and felt emotionally closer to his girl friend.

At this point, the satisfaction he was getting from his new sex life seemed more therapeutic than anything I could offer, so I suggested a two-month vacation from therapy. At the end of this period, Arthur reported that he was free of his problem. He still had an occasional homosexual fantasy, but it was without emotional intensity. He was now living with a new girl friend, and for the first time in his life thought he was falling in love.

How, when, or why Arthur had learned to excite himself by thinking of naked men had never been a factor in treating this case. It was obvious that the habit had become so fixed that he could not break it on his own. Aversion treatment helped him do this, and aversion relief aided in the transfer of pleasant sexual feelings to women. The removal of his disturbing habit and the assertive training allowed him to express his feelings more spontaneously. In any event, Arthur is more satisfied with himself and his life.

Aversive shocks have also been administered with favorable results in the treatment of compulsive gambling. Drs. J. C. Barker and M. B. Miller, British therapists, had a patient who was pathologically unable to stay out of London horse parlors. When the amount of time and money he was devoting to bookmakers became intolerable to him, he went for help. The therapists had him followed for days by a camera crew, who filmed him at the track placing bets at the tote window and the bookie stalls, and at off-track bookmakers' wire rooms betting on races at American and Australian tracks at hours when English racing was over. When the film was first screened for the patient, he was given a microphone and told to record his thoughts while watching himself in action.

For six weeks our gambler was forced to watch himself daily while the familiar sounds of the track and bookie stalls mingled with his own comments. At unexpected moments he got strong shocks. Long before the six weeks were up he was sick of the whole thing. A two-year follow-up found that he had given up gambling.

Barker and Miller used real-life stimuli in treating a slot-machine addict. This compulsive gambler spent many nights, feeding shillings to the one-armed bandit until he could hardly stand. The therapists hospitalized him so that treatment could be properly supervised, borrowed a slot machine from the local pub, and hooked up the patient to a seventy-volt induction coil. The patient had been playing the machines for twelve years, and he was determined to give up the practice for good.

He was first given 150 random shocks during a three-hour period, the length of his usual session with the slot machine. The jolts came at random—while he was feeding in the coins, when he pulled down the lever, while the lemons, oranges, and bells whirled before him, or during the infrequent payoffs. During the final twelve-hour session (he was shocked nearly seven hundred times) he was ready to quit after the first six hours, but the therapists instructed him to continue inserting coins and pulling the lever. He didn't gamble again for a year and a half. After a brief relapse, a booster session of six hours was enough to restore the aversion.

One drawback of the aversive methods in general is the need for a high level of motivation on the part of the patient. The aversive effects can easily generalize to the treatment situation itself and cause the patient to reject all therapy. However, if his motivation is strong enough he will be able to tolerate painful electric shocks without trying to back out.

A drawback of the shock technique itself is the fact that it is usually performed in a hospital or the therapist's office. The patient who has just been freed of an unwanted habit fears that the habit will return. It is not always convenient for him to see his therapist for booster treatment. The ex-homosexual, for instance, may unexpectedly find himself face to face with an old roommate, and feel the need of a booster shock to help him resist temptation.

Equipment manufacturers have produced a hand shocker that a patient may carry in his pocket to give himself aversive treatment.

Wolpe* writes of a physician who started taking Demerol to carry him over an emotional crisis and became addicted, still taking it several years later when he felt no anxiety. He was given a portable shocker and was able to give himself a jolt whenever he felt the craving coming on, enabling him to control the craving. It would be of great help if this form of treatment were effective with drug addicts in general, but the necessary studies have not yet been made.

The portable faradic apparatus is not inexpensive. A reasonably priced substitute can be purchased for about two dollars at novelty stores that sell magic apparatus and practical jokes. The item appears to be a plastic box about the size and shape of a playing-card case, bearing a reproduction of an erotic playing card. When the jokester's victim tries to open the box, he gets a shock. The shock is strong enough to serve the purpose of a patient needing do-it-yourself aversion treatment between sessions. I always caution the patient, however, to replace the battery as it runs down. A weak shock can reinforce unwanted habits.

The use of aversive shocks in treating the problems of youngsters will be discussed in Chapter 9.

Despite the widespread use of electric shock, it is relatively new to the field of aversion treatment. The first aversive stimuli were chemicals which were used primarily in an experimental way during early investigation of the treatment of alcoholism.

Drug-induced aversion therapy was pioneered by Drs. F. Lemere and W. L. Voegtlin in the 1940s. The alcoholic

---

* *The Practice of Behavior Therapy,* by Joseph Wolpe, M.D.

was injected with some emetic compound such as apo-morphine, and then offered a drink or two. He was to savor the whiskey slowly, to appreciate its bouquet and flavor, so that he would associate them with the violent nausea which the emetic would produce.

The two therapists indicated they had had excellent short-term results. Of their first 1200 patients, 75 percent abstained completely for two years. The longer-term picture, while positive, is less encouraging. Out of some 4100 patients, about 40 percent were still abstemious after five years, while 23 percent had still not touched a drink ten years or more after their aversive treatment.

In general the drug approach is being abandoned as an aversive technique because the timing of its effect is so hard to control. The principle of aversive therapy—the simultaneous or nearly simultaneous association of the un-wanted stimulus with an unpleasant, punitive effect—is not followed in the Lemere-Voegtlin methods. The patient has had time to be turned on by the pleasant smell, taste, and pervasive warmth of the whiskey before he is turned off by the unpleasant nausea of the emetic. Thus the stimulus (alcohol) is first followed by a positive reinforcement (the smell and taste) and only later is the negative reinforce-ment (the shock) experienced. Under these conditions a habit will be maintained and strengthened rather than sup-pressed. The control of timing makes faradic aversion so superior to chemical aversion.

An easily applied aversion technique that meets our criteria for timing is called *thought-stopping*. This method is quite effective when applied to patients who are tense because of an anxiety-producing train of unrealistic thought that persists to the point of obsession.

Thought-stopping worked very well, for example, with Alice W. Alice was an ambitious young woman who held a responsible position with an important law firm. She took her work seriously and saw a successful career before her. Her problem: she could not sleep at night.

As soon as she got to bed the events of the day started whirling through her mind like autumn leaves in a high wind. She became more and more tense as the hours dragged by. She remembered things she should have left unsaid, others she could have said better, situations she might have handled better. By midnight she was wide awake. Sleep seemed out of the question.

We tried the relaxation routine but her SUD level remained high. Then I decided to try thought-stopping, a technique first suggested in the twenties by J. Alexander Bain and developed by J. G. Taylor in the fifties. Alice lay on the couch with her eyes closed. I told her to picture herself in bed about to go to sleep. She was to signal as soon as she became aware of the thoughts starting to come.

As soon as she signaled, I shouted loudly, "Stop!"

Alice was obviously startled. She jumped. Her eyes opened. Then we repeated the going-to-sleep scene.

This time it took a little longer for the unwelcome thoughts to move in. When she signaled, I shouted "Stop!" and reinforced my shout by banging on the metal filing cabinet beside me.

The third time around the shout of "Stop!" was accompanied by the blast of a portable Freon foghorn—the type used on small power boats. The horn really shook her. When I repeated the scene, she had trouble imagining the sleep-killing thought. The foghorn was definitely aversive. The next time she became aware of the thoughts first crowding in, she herself shouted "Stop!" as loudly as she could. Eventually she was to shout silently to herself.

I told her when she went to bed that night, she should mentally shout "Stop!" at herself the moment the disturbing train of thought began its usual intrusion. At her next session she reported that the memory of the raucous blast of the Freon horn which accompanied her silent shout of "Stop!" had successfully blocked off the anxiety-provoking thoughts. She had learned to fall asleep.

The foghorn was not needed for a family friend of mine who was flying to Europe for her annual visit and was terrified by the prospect of flying. She always needed at least a week to recover from the torture of the few hours in the air. She spent the entire flight worrying about what might happen if the plane should be disabled over the Atlantic. What if it should be hit by lightning? Would it disintegrate? Suppose they were forced to ditch? Would she be able to reach a life raft? What if the life raft should upset? Would she be rescued before she perished of exposure? Was drowning a lingering and difficult way to die?

This woman was not a patient, so I did not give her the full aversive treatment. I merely gave her some friendly advice on how to use aversive therapy as a do-it-yourself means of getting rid of her fears in flight. She was to shout "Stop!"—silently, of course—when thoughts of catastrophe began to spoil her trip.

A few months later she telephoned to thank me for a wonderful vacation. "I shouted to myself to stop," she said, "and I slept most of the way across, both coming and going."

Few patients with obsessive anxiety-producing thought patterns respond as quickly and simply as the two women whose cases I have just described. However, conditioning a patient to connect an unpleasant association with compulsive thinking can be accomplished in many cases with persistence and patience.

Aversive therapy has also been successful in countering compulsive *actions* by unpleasant association. The pioneer of this method, called *covert sensitization,* is Dr. Joseph R. Cautela of Boston College. Since Dr. Cautela provides the aversive stimulus through imagery, he must first find out what concept to present that will be most repulsive to the patient. Vomit seems a singularly disgusting stimulus. Although originally used as an inhibitory concept in treating compulsive eaters and obesity, it has proved effective for many other compulsions. Take the case of Albert Q.

Al was a compulsive automobile thief. A normal youth in all other respects, he simply could not walk past an unoccupied parked car if the owner had left his keys in the ignition. He felt compelled to get in and drive it away. There was no profit motive involved; he never tried to sell the stolen car. He merely drove it as fast and as far as it would go before it ran out of gas or into a tree. It was a court that committed him to psychotherapy, but Albert himself wanted to break this habit.

After trying several other approaches first, I resorted to covert sensitization. As Albert lay on the couch with his eyes closed, I instructed:

"Picture yourself walking along the street. You see a brand-new shiny Lincoln Continental parked at the curb. You walk closer and notice the key has been left in the ignition. There is nobody around, so you try the door handle. The door opens. You get in. The red-leather upholstery, the whole interior, smells new. You have a queasy feeling. As you close the door behind you the feeling gets worse. You slide behind the wheel, and the nausea mounts. You try to keep it down, but as you reach forward to turn the key, you lose control. Whoops, there it comes!"

At this point I summon up whatever histrionic ability I possess to produce the sound effects of violent retching. The realism almost backfires on me.

"You're throwing up all over yourself." More retching sounds. "All over your new suit. Your necktie is a mess. The sour stink makes you even sicker. You're leaning over the wheel and the leather upholstery is slippery with your vomit." More sound effects. "You can't stop. You feel the slimy wetness through your shirt. It seems as if you've thrown up most of your guts, yet you still gag and retch. There's nothing left but the bitter taste in your mouth. You feel you must get out of this car. You stumble out the door. You seem to have left that acrid smell of vomit behind you. You breathe deeply, and the nausea has gone. The slimy wetness, too, has disappeared. You walk away from that Continental, faster and faster. You feel good again."

We do this routine daily, for a while, varying the scene somewhat until Al never wants to see another car with the key carelessly left behind to tempt him. Then I give him a tape recording to take home and play back if he begins to have fantasies about stealing another car.

I have used covert sensitization successfully in a case of potential alcoholism. The patient was a businessman who thought a three-martini lunch was essential to maintaining important contacts. He rationalized his evening libations by saying they were necessary to help him unwind after a hard day at the office. He had drunk himself into a case of severe gastritis with incipient ulcers, and his physician had ordered him to stop drinking entirely.

He had followed the doctor's orders faithfully, and had avoided all alcohol. He could not, however, get rid of the craving. He was haunted by fantasies of the friendly cocktail, the pleasant aroma of good whiskey, the warming taste of a postprandial brandy. When he could stand it no longer, he came to me for help.

Covert sensitization seemed indicated, and inasmuch as he had been frightened by the bloody vomit caused by his gastritis, the vomiting stimulus seemed made to order. Together we drew up the scenario. It was an exaggeration of his own experience, with all the disgusting details larger than life. The patient could imagine the alcoholic details without further damage to his digestive system. After the first session, we made a tape which he took home with him to play whenever he started dreaming of three-martini luncheons and the scotch sour after his Sunday-morning golf.

Within a week, his fantasies were 70 percent gone. Within two weeks they were 99 percent gone. The last time I heard from him he had craved no alcohol for three months.

Covert sensitization is particularly useful because it can be done at home with the aid of a tape recorder. Since the therapist can make the tape, there is much better control over the timing of the aversion than with the hand shocker, which depends only on the patient for the timing.

One of the psychological advantages of the covert-conditioning technique is the direct participation of the patient in his own therapy. Dr. Cautela tells me he makes full use of the patient in preparing the aversive stimulus for office therapy and for home treatment. This stimulus is a highly personalized matter and must be tailored to fit each individual. While vomitus and vermin are fairly universal in their repellent effect, some patients have to be turned off by rats, mice, snakes, spiders, or feces.

Dr. Cautela actually has the patient dictate the scene at home, aversion and all, and then bring the tape into the office for the therapist to check. The patient can custom tailor these scenes for himself better than anyone else can —and he gets that extra dose of aversion while making the tape.

Aversion treatment has also been tried for stopping the cigarette habit. Many different approaches have been used, some with a modicum of success. One, which must be limited to individuals in good physical condition, can be described as follows:

Several nights a week the person trying to shake the habit enters the bathroom with a large ashtray and a pack of his favorite cigarettes. The door and windows must be tightly closed. The first step is to light six or seven cigarettes and to let them burn on the edge of the ashtray, so that the air is soon blue with smoke. The tobacco addict then tries to chain-smoke seven cigarettes in quick succession, ending within fifteen minutes. The smoke-filled bathroom combined with the rapid smoking can be most aversive.

This method, like the others, has been effective on occasion, but usually only temporarily. Nonsmoking behavior is very hard to maintain beyond short periods.

Personally, I do not treat cigarette fiends. I have tried to break the habit by covert sensitization only once, and I failed. The patient? Myself.

7

THE INCOMPLETE MALE: *Treating*
Impotence and Premature Ejaculation

TREATMENT OF MALE sexual problems dramatically illustrates the difference between the approaches of psychoanalysts and behavior therapists. Analysts say that men's
most common sexual problems, impotence and premature
ejaculation, are very often caused by Oedipal complexes,
fantasies involving forbidden thoughts, and similar deep-
seated influences. In some instances they may be right, but
whether they are or are not is irrelevant to behavior therapy. The behavior therapist is not interested in prime
causes. He is concerned with the fact that in some manner
—perhaps quite accidentally—anxiety has come to influence
the man's sexual behavior.

Freudian literature does not deal with the concept of
accidentally acquired symptoms, but we know that accidental learning does take place. Symptoms also can be accidentally learned. The classic example is the case of the
young husband who found himself impotent scarcely six
months after his marriage. As reported by French psychiatrist Prof. P. Meignant, the honeymoon had been sexually
successful for both partners. When the newlyweds settled
in a home that the bride herself had redecorated, the groom
suddenly discovered he was sexually incompetent. His problem had continued, with few temporary "relapses" into
virility, until he decided to come for help.

The therapist was interested in the remissions. The

patient remembered that his virility had returned temporarily several times: during the winter when they had impulsively made love on a rug in front of the fire, and when they went away together on summer weekends. Only in the bedroom was the husband psychologically emasculated. What was causing the problem?

The therapist eventually discovered that the root of the man's impotence lay in a conditioned reflex he had acquired without even knowing it. Several years before his marriage, the groom had had an affair with a married woman. One day her husband had made an unexpected entrance at a moment of tender intimacy. The violent scene that followed apparently had a lasting traumatic effect.

Seeking to connect this premarital scene with the patient's present marital difficulties, the therapist's questions focused on the bedroom: what inhibiting factor could it possibly contain? Systematic examination finally revealed the vital clues. The wallpaper his bride had selected for their bedroom was almost an exact replica of that which had decorated the bedroom where his love affair had been ended by the furious husband. The newlyweds' bedroom was repapered and the sexual problem disappeared.

In discussing this case, some of my analysis-oriented colleagues insisted that the traumatic bedroom scene was merely an unconscious re-enactment of the Oedipal situation. The irate husband represented the father. The violent confrontation symbolized the patricide, the wife the forbidden object—and the postnuptial sexual collapse was obviously a castration situation. The man's basic problem was still unresolved.

This explanation is based on the assumption that there was a "basic problem," beyond the man's sexual inadequacy. The behavior therapist's simple application of the laws of learning led to an understanding of the man's impotence without any such assumption. A simple change of the stimulus (i.e., the wallpaper) brought about the desired change in behavior, and the married couple had a happier life. The case can be explained best in terms of the man's having learned a symptom accidentally.

Among the men who have come to see me about their sexual problems, the greatest single cause of impotence is the fear of failure to attain or maintain an erection. Masters and Johnson, as a result of their research in human sexual behavior, conclude (and the italics are theirs): *"It should be restated that the fear of inadequacy is the greatest known deterrent to effective sexual functioning."* Effective sexual function, they explain, is a natural reaction to sexual stimulation. When a person worries about his performance ability, he blocks out the sexual stimuli so the natural reaction does not take place. The step-by-step procedures Masters and Johnson have developed to remove fears of inadequacy and heighten sexual stimulation are basically those used in behavior therapy, as the authors themselves acknowledge.

However, the Masters-Johnson techniques are not automatically or universally applicable. Not every sexual problem is based on fear of inadequacy, and careful behavioral diagnosis is always required. Other fears are sometimes involved and may be dealt with by techniques useful in treating phobias. In the case of fear of pain, we must first get a medical opinion as to whether or not the sexual act actually is painful.

I have seen three or four male patients in which pain seemed to be involved. One of them was a twenty-six-year-old French Canadian whom we will call Pierre. Pierre was a likable, effusive graduate student who seemed to be in good control of his life. He was in love with a fellow student and wanted to marry her, but he had a serious handicap: he was incapable of sexual intercourse.

Pierre had tried to overcome his problem, but he was

119

still technically a virgin. His fiancée was ready and willing, and excited him to the point of erection. Before he could accomplish penetration, however, his erection was gone.

Pierre's problem dated back to his birth. He was born with a foreskin that was too tight for his penis. When he was old enough to get an erection, the tight foreskin caused him pain. When he began to masturbate, he experienced more pain at the point of ejaculation. He had tried intercourse—without success, because the pain destroyed his erection.

Several years before he came to see me, his family physician recommended circumcision. He had complied. As a result of losing his foreskin, he no longer experienced pain in the penis, but he was still left with the anticipation of pain. He also interpreted other sensations as pain. For instance, the simple pressure of water from the shower striking his genitals was painful to him.

The diagnostic picture was clear, and treatment through nonsystematic desensitization began during his first visit. Pierre was relaxed and told to picture the worst possible tension-evoking sexual scenes. He was to signal the first sign of any disturbed feeling, whereupon we would stop the visualization and he would be relaxed again. We went through this routine twenty-five times during the session. He was so thoroughly conditioned to anticipate pain in this situation that during the first scenes he reported that he actually did feel pain in his penis. With repetition the pain diminished. When he left my office, he told me he had a date with his fiancée that night, and I wished him luck.

Next morning the telephone woke me at the crack of dawn. It was Pierre, almost shouting, "It worked, Doc! It worked!" For the first time in his life he had been able to enjoy normal sexual relations with a woman.

Pierre came back a number of times to complete the desensitization process before he was discharged. He phoned me six months later to report that everything was still going well, and that he was getting married.

I have seen many cases of idiosyncratic sexual difficulties in which the generalization of other fears and phobias have affected a man's virility. One of these was that of Gordon T., who had enjoyed perfectly normal sexual relations before his marriage, but was incapable of intercourse with his new wife, whom he loved dearly. He had undergone no physical change since the wedding; he could still function with prostitutes.

In talking with Gordon, I found that he had a mild case of claustrophobia. He was uneasy in airplanes and mildly frightened in crowded elevators. He was afraid of being trapped and of suffocating. The fear of entrapment was extended to marriage, and his reluctance to commit himself completely to his wife made him impotent.

Once I had diagnosed the source of Gordon's trouble, I prepared a series of imaginary scenes to desensitize him to his particular type of claustrophobia. Since fear of suffocation was involved, I had him picture a number of scenes in which he was unable to catch his breath while making love to his wife. Eventually he was able to visualize the situation without tension, and later, to his wife's delight, successfully shed his anxiety in bed.

Another patient of mine, who was impotent only part of the time, did not realize that his real trouble was that he was afraid of the dark. Once we were able to establish the time of his sexual successes, which indicated he had no difficulty maintaining an erection in the daytime or when the light was on, we worked out a desensitization series for nyctophobia.

Fear may psychologically emasculate otherwise virile males, and wreck the best of sexual plans. I have seen men whose primary phobia was a fear of bright light, of noise, of a woman's excitement, of having a heart attack, of losing control—even of beds. Some type of deconditioning (desensitization) is usually effective in treating sexual inadequacy.

At the beginning of this chapter, I indicated that the most frequent cause of male impotence was the fear of failure to have an erection. How does the behavior therapist treat this fear? Usually, he uses systematic desensitization, as described in Chapter 3. The anxiety-provoking scenes to be visualized are essentially the same as described by Dr. Arnold A. Lazarus, formerly of Temple University Medical School, currently at Yale, in his treatise on group therapy for impotent men.*

Dr. Lazarus discusses his treatment of three men: A., age 28; B., 26; and C., 32. A. had had a few successful sexual experiences in his life, but none for some years. B. had never had a complete erection. C. was intermittently potent during the first eight years of his marriage, but had not been during the past year. All three men were constantly afraid of sexual failure.

Most of the first session was devoted to instruction in basic anatomy, a subject on which most men display amazing ignorance. To explain the physiology of erection, I prefer the analogy I use to get the attention of a sleepy early-morning class of residents in psychiatry. Do you know the difference, I ask, between the love life of horses and that of cattle? Horses indulge in a great deal of foreplay, while cattle have none. Why? Because of the structural difference between the penis of a stallion and that of the bull. The bull's organ derives its firmness from a cartilage structure, is always ready, and needs only to be unsheathed. The stallion, on the other hand, has a penis of a spongelike vascular nature that requires an influx of blood to be en-

* In *Basic Approaches to Group Therapy*, edited by George Gazba.

larged and stiffened—like a man's. In man, amorous preliminaries stimulate the blood flow. Anxiety impedes it.

The Lazarus group was also taught how to bring a woman to climax by means other than coitus, such as stimulation of the clitoris, digital manipulation, and cunnilingus. The session ended with fifteen minutes of muscular relaxation training.

The three wives attended the first part of the second session to learn how their cooperation would be of great help in restoring their husbands' virility. One of them objected to the proposed direct clitoral stimulation, but agreed to try it when it was explained that the practice was quite normal, that it was only temporary, and that her participation in intimate sexual foreplay was essential to her husband's therapy.

The rest of the session was devoted to relaxation of the husbands to an even greater degree than they had been previously relaxed. They were also reminded to focus on giving utmost sexual pleasure to their partners by a variety of methods.

The third session was devoted to systematic desensitization. The husbands were put through the process of deep relaxation followed by visualization of scenes that had previously caused tension. The scenes they were to picture were:

> Kissing the wife
> Petting while fully dressed
> Undressing
> Love play in the nude
> Preparation for copulation
> Change of position during coition

The presentations were made several times for periods ranging from five to thirty seconds. Later the time devoted to the final scenes was lengthened to sixty seconds. One man had trouble visualizing the change in positions during intercourse, and was given individual therapy for a week.

At the end of the course, all three men were successful sexually. B. credited the desensitization routine with having made him virile again. The other two men credited the cooperation of their wives. C. reported two years later that he had been having erections regularly.

In office practice the therapist's presentation of the scenes for visualization are tape-recorded so that the patient may take them home and continue his active participation in his own therapy.

When the patient moves from picturing the therapist's scenes to their actual enactment, the cooperation of the wife becomes all-important. Her helpfulness, patience, and understanding can make or break the program of revitalization.

The principle involved in restoring sexual potency is to reduce tension on the one hand and to heighten sexual enjoyment on the other. Tension is reduced by temporarily forbidding intercourse, which is really what frightens the man. Sexual stimulation is heightened by encouraging frequent and intense love play. The instructions to the couple are to make this sex play as exciting and fulfilling as possible for each other and themselves—without intercourse. As enjoyment increases, erections usually increase accordingly, and the fear of inadequacy therefore disappears. Once the man is fairly confident of maintaining his erection, he may then go on to coitus.

Many men have resolved sexual difficulties through this method, with the enthusiastic cooperation of a concerned woman.

Sometimes, a more gradual approach may be necessary. Progressive steps leading toward coitus, but avoiding it initially, are aimed at removing the tension which may develop at each stage. The steps may be:

Lying quietly in each other's arms
The wife caressing the man, but not below the navel
The wife fondling the man's penis for five minutes
The wife fondling the penis for fifteen minutes

If tension develops during any stage, the exercise is stopped immediately and the couple rests and relaxes. Each step is continued until no tension is experienced in three repeated trials. The exercise must never continue to the point of ejaculation. In fact, the caresses and love play must be kept separate from the idea of intercourse until all anxiety has been extinguished in the husband.

When the husband is able to maintain his erection for long enough to contemplate entry, he lets his wife take over. The husband should be lying on his back, with his wife kneeling astride to manage the penetration. There should be no attempt at coital movement, no actual coitus. This is merely an exercise to determine whether the husband is able to maintain an erection to the point of approaching copulation without anxiety or tension. If there is any tension along the way, he goes back a step and starts over.

When he feels that he is ready at last for intercourse, he may find that the first ejaculation will be without emotion. The orgasm will be physical, but without the overwhelming orgasmic involvement that he might expect. But the emotional reaction will soon come as the anxiety continues to decrease.

What do we do if the patient is unmarried and has no sympathetic girl friend who will help him during the initial stages of his therapy? The role of the woman is essential in dealing with an impotent male. Fortunately, there are many women ready to help in solving a man's sexual problems. There are also many men who are so up tight about women that we must rely on professional talent.

Many men, who would find it impossible to undergo the treatment I have suggested with a woman they know, feel quite different about it if they can pay the woman for her help. In New York City there are a number of professional prostitutes—and some semiprofessionals who have other jobs—who are willing to undertake this type of work. I insist that the professional partner must telephone me for instructions before each appointment so that the exercises may be properly supervised. On several occasions I have had to advise the patient to leave his partner and find a new one. Usually, however, they are very cooperative, and gain a great deal of satisfaction as they see a patient improve. At all times I remind the patient that this form of treatment is temporary; when it becomes possible, he should transfer his sexual activity to a more personal relationship. I have never had any difficulty in effecting this transfer, once the patient has become sexually confident.

One of my patients who needed help of this sort was Gerald M., a shy young man in his early twenties. Gerald held a master's degree in business administration and filled a responsible job as the administrator of an antipoverty project. He lived at home with his father and a sister, which may have had something to do with his fear of women. He never dated girls because he was terrified that one would expect him to go to bed with her and would find him inadequate.

We started on the prescribed course of relaxation and desensitization, and Gerald seemed to be making better than average progress. He found a professional partner and I devised a systematic program for them, one that took into account Gerald's terror of women.

Their first meetings took place in a coffeehouse. The

rules called for them to avoid the subject of sex for the first three meetings. Any other topic of conversation—New York, politics, the movies—was all right. At the fourth meeting, the girl was told to bring up the subject of sex in an impersonal and indirect way.

The fifth meeting—at the girl's apartment—was to be purely platonic. Gerald was allowed to kiss her good night, but nothing more. Petting with clothes on was stretched over the next three meetings and was followed by several sessions of petting in the nude. To overcome Gerald's extreme naïveté and to minimize his tension, the girl was instructed to play the role of teacher, giving Gerald lessons in practical anatomy. By tutoring him in the techniques of sex she led him step by step toward intercourse. All three of us felt great triumph at his first successful consummation.

With his fear of sexual inadequacy gone, his terror of women also disappeared. He is now able not only to date but to form increasingly close relationships with women.

The use of a prostitute was also part of my treatment for a homosexual patient who had been turned off by his fear of women. Although he wanted to remain homosexual, one of his therapeutic goals was freedom to engage in heterosexual activities as well. I have dealt more thoroughly with homosexuality in Chapter 6, but I mention this case because of its connection with the fear of women.

The program designed for him was essentially the same as the one planned for Gerald. However, in this instance the fear of women was not as great and progress was more rapid. Aided by systematic desensitization through imagery, he soon became involved in a more personal relationship with a woman friend. A year later he indicated that he was quite satisfied with his bisexuality.

One of my patients, a high-ranking foreign service officer we will call Pennington, was deeply in love with a woman whom he wanted to marry. He was very much afraid, however, that he could never consummate the marriage. He was capable of an occasional erection, but could not maintain one long enough for satisfactory intercourse. His feelings of sexual competence had been completely undermined by his ex-wife, who was both frigid and hostile. He had been undergoing traditional therapy for some time, but was making little progress and could get no encouraging prognosis from his analyst. Understandably impatient, he came to see me.

Pennington was due to go overseas in a few months to attend a conference in an Eastern European country, and he didn't want to lose any time. We held extra sessions in relaxation and desensitization, and I prepared tapes he could take abroad with him to play in his hotel room.

I chuckled as I imagined Pennington in his hotel room (bugged, of course) turning on his tape recorder. I laughed aloud when I thought of the secret police trying to decipher the hidden meaning of the voice saying:

"Picture yourself lying in bed with your girl friend Margaret. You are both nude, and are lying very close to one another. Picture this as vividly as you can. You reach out for Margaret and take her into your arms. . . . Stop the scene."

Fortunately the problem never developed. Pennington's sexual difficulty cleared up before he went overseas, thanks in part to the desensitization tapes, thanks more particularly to the sympathetic understanding and cooperation of his fiancée.

A less than understanding sexual partner—a domineering wife, for instance—can be a prime cause of impotence in men. The henpecked husband is a major candidate for sexual inadequacy, but the treatment is different from that for the fear of not maintaining an erection, fear of women, or some other phobia not directly connected with sex. It is assertive training.

The characteristics of assertion have been discussed in Chapter 4. The influence of assertive problems on sexual behavior may be general or specific, but it is always considerable. The man who feels pushed around by his wife tends to develop resentment, anger, or depression—all of which interfere with his sexual functions. Making love to a woman with whom he is angry is difficult, if not impossible, and depression is notorious for decreasing sexual drive.

The specific problems have to do with communication and the expression of his feelings in approaching sex. He cannot confide his likes and dislikes to his wife and so may find sex unsatisfactory. He may have difficulty expressing his tenderness and excitement and so minimize the enjoyment and spontaneity of sex. Coition, after all, is an assertive act. Assertive training is the answer to his specific difficulties.

If the problem is a general one, the man must be taught to stand up to his wife. Here, too, he must learn to communicate his feelings, his likes and dislikes. Assertive-training techniques like behavior rehearsal and assertive phrases —as well as other behavioral methods, such as desensitization—will help him become the complete male.

After impotence, the most common sexual problem among males is premature ejaculation. The psychological effect is the same as in the case of impotence: his partner is left with a feeling of frustration, and the man with the same sense of failure.

We must always be sure that the problem is really premature ejaculation. One man came to me in a state of despair. He was a young stockbroker I will call Downey, a sensitive, considerate husband of a year's standing. He was troubled by a continuous history of premature ejaculation, which left him with a feeling of guilt and inadequacy, and his wife with a sense of unfulfillment. As a result a good deal of tension was developing in an otherwise warm, satisfactory marriage relationship.

Downey and his wife had indulged in premarital sex, but neither had had intercourse with a third party. Even their premarital relations were not entirely satisfactory.

Questioning of Downey revealed that he had no difficulty in achieving and maintaining an erection. His only problem was that he ejaculated before his wife achieved climax, regardless of the amount of foreplay or the intensity of her excitement before penetration. The clinical picture indicated that the problem might be the wife's frigidity (despite her orgasmic response to manual clitoral stimulation) rather than Downey's premature ejaculation.

To test this theory, I told Downey that the next few times he went to bed with his wife he should count the number of strokes he took before ejaculating, to report to me. The answer was thirty-six. Whether his movement was continuous or intermittent, the thirty-sixth stroke always triggered an orgasm. When I asked what he meant by intermittent, he explained that he could interrupt coitus at almost any point before his three-dozen-stroke limit and maintain an erection for as long as half an hour inside his wife's vagina.

Downey's problem called for a two-level approach. I desensitized Downey to his wife's dissatisfaction, and I put Mrs. Downey through a course of desensitization for her residual frigidity. They finally achieved mutual satisfaction in bed.

From the behavioral perspective, premature ejaculation stems from one of three conditions, each of which requires a different treatment. First, there may be a physiological hypersensitivity of the penis which leads to a rapid climax. This is treated by reducing the sensitivity. Second and most commonly, the man may simply have been trained to ejaculate quickly. He must be retrained. Finally, anxiety may have become associated with sex, producing quick ejaculation. For this condition, one of the tension-reduction methods—general relaxation or systematic desensitization, perhaps—may be the treatment of choice.

Physiological sensitivity may be reduced in a number of ways. Counting strokes, which I suggested for Downey, will often delay the climax and build up tolerance. If it does not, we resort to physical means. An ointment containing a mild local anesthetic can be applied to the penis prior to intercourse, and this will slow down the approach to orgasm. Any physician will prescribe one of the several mild ointments available. Wearing a condom—or two or three condoms to be shed one at a time as tolerance is built up—is another alternative.

For the man who ejaculates with a flaccid organ or before penetration these methods will obviously not work, because the reduction of stimulation to the penis may interfere with the maintenance of an erection.

Some men's sexual problems may call for the retraining technique, which is actually a form of discipline. It, too, requires the active cooperation of the wife, who may not find her role easy. She must be patient, for there is no actual intercourse during the training period, although the husband may satisfy her by other means.

Initially, both husband and wife are given detailed instructions for the behavioral procedure they should follow at home. After disrobing as usual and indulging in amatory preliminaries for a while, the wife starts to fondle her husband's genitalia. She continues until he feels the premonitory signs of ejaculation and signals her to stop. It is extremely important that this signal be given at the *first approach* of ejaculatory sensation. If she continues, orgasm becomes inevitable.

When the husband signals, one of two courses of action

must be immediately followed. Masters and Johnson describe a technique which involves pinching the head of the penis to stop the ejaculatory feelings. The other method is simply to relax and allow the feelings to subside completely. In either case, when the sensation is completely gone, the wife resumes fondling her husband's penis, and the process is repeated. It may be repeated four, five, or more times a night.

It is important that either husband or wife—probably the wife, since she seems to be in charge of the program at this point—keep track of the time that elapses until the preejaculatory feelings appear. The longer the interval, 'the more progress the husband is making. With repetition on the same day, the interval may grow progressively shorter, but on subsequent days it will eventually grow longer. When the patient is able to tolerate the pleasant stimulation for twenty minutes before the preliminary stages of orgasm are felt, he is ready for the next step.

Step Two involves the use of a lubricant. The penis becomes more sensitive when ointment is applied, so when the wife uses a cream for her erotic manipulations, the critical interval will probably drop sharply. It will grow longer, however, if the routine followed in Step One—breaking off before ejaculation, resting until excitement has drained from the genitalia, then starting again—is followed in Step Two as well.

The next step is penetration. Once the erogenous preliminaries have made him physically prepared, the husband lies flat on his back. His wife then kneels astride him, facilitates entry into her vagina, and remains motionless. At the first sign of pre-ejaculatory sensation, her husband signals her to get off. At this point she may try the Masters-Johnson pinch technique, or both may just relax until his feelings subside. The process is then repeated. At first the husband may signal for a halt only a few seconds after penetration, but the second or third time the interval will increase. When he can stay inside her for fifteen or twenty minutes without an orgasm, he is ready to attempt a little movement—still without ejaculating.

In the final stage the husband takes over. He enters from above and remains inside the vagina until he feels the approaching climax, then withdraws. When the critical interval lengthens beyond a quarter hour, he will find himself instinctively sliding into normal coitus—without premature ejaculation.

Worry, as I have indicated earlier, is the most frequent cause of sexual inadequacy in men. Although nonsexual worries—financial troubles, loss of a job, concern over the health of someone close—have a distinctly negative effect on sexual performance, anxiety about effective performance causes most of the trouble.

Fear of failure can become obsessive. A married man can worry all day whether his wife will be in the mood for sex that night. Will he disappoint her? Will she be frustrated if he is unable to get an erection, or if he does, will she be frustrated by his shortcomings? Anxiety grows as bedtime approaches, and too often his fears become a self-fulfilling prophecy.

Systematic desensitization against such anxieties is very much the same for both impotence and premature ejaculation: relaxation, followed by visualizations of tension-provoking scenes: kissing, petting, undressing, caressing, going to bed, nestling in each other's arms, nude love play, coitus. At each stage during therapy, the patient signals rising tension, and we start over.

All this may seem oversimplified, but it is not simple. Sometimes many sessions—in the therapist's office and at home—are necessary before the seemingly impotent male is able to picture the approach to copulation without anxiety. There is no magic involved in reconditioning him to regard going to bed with a woman as a joyous adventure rather than an ordeal. All that is usually required is a combination of patience and the proper psychological training.

8

THE DISTURBED WOMAN: *What to Do About Frigidity and Promiscuity*

FROM HER APPEARANCE as she walked into my study, the woman didn't seem to have a care in the world. She was in her mid-thirties, attractive, well groomed, and, judging from her poise and her speech, sophisticated. Yet she had come to consult me about a problem that had worried her for years: she was sexually frigid.

Hers was not a case of primary frigidity, a condition I will discuss later in this chapter. A woman who had been married for fifteen years and had borne three children, she had achieved orgasm, but never during sexual intercourse. Could she be helped?

Mrs. R. had spent several years in psychoanalysis trying to deal with her handicap, but without success. She wanted to know what behavior therapy could do for her. The behavior therapist, as I have indicated, is not interested in possible causes arising from the unconscious; he merely wants to determine what the patient has learned wrong, which is now causing her problem.

Although Mrs. R. had never reached a climax during coitus, she was familiar with the orgasmic experience. She had been brought to the physical peak of excitement through caressing the clitoris. Since Mrs. R. was physically capable of reaching orgasm, couldn't her reflexes be reconditioned so that she could do so during coition?

The first step was to determine whether anxiety kept

her from sexual fulfillment. My discussions with her indicated that it did. Her Calvinistic upbringing still played an important part in her attitude toward sex. Her moralistic parents were strict disciplinarians who believed that life was a long series of temptations to be resisted. Sex was a nasty business to be tolerated only within the holy bonds of matrimony, and then solely for the purpose of procreation. It was never to be mentioned by decent women and only the most depraved men spoke of it in mixed company.

With maturity and marriage Mrs. R. began to realize that there was more to life than was encompassed within the stern horizon of her parents. Still, she had been so well trained to regard sex as loathsome that she could not escape her childhood conditioning. Even the four-letter words so common in "respectable" books read by her friends still shocked her. Her reaction to these words was so strong that I decided to use them as an integral part of her therapy. Hopefully any change in her reaction to the words would be generalized to change her entire emotional attitude toward sex.

Mrs. R. and I sat down to draw up a list of the words that still caused her anxiety. We then put them on index cards and arranged them in an order of ascending "shock" value—a hierarchy for systematic desensitization. I then relaxed her and began reading the "obscenities." She was to raise a finger whenever she felt tension, and I would relax her again. When she was relaxed I would repeat the word that had increased her anxiety.

The list consisted of twenty-three words ranging from breast and buttocks to prick, cunt, and fuck. Each word was read to her until she could hear it twice in succession without feeling any tension. We needed several sessions to go through the entire list.

When she could remain relaxed while listening to the

lubricious vocabulary, I asked her to put the words into sentences she might hear from her husband during lovemaking, and later, sentences she might address to him in bed. They are not hard to imagine. Twenty years ago they would have appeared in print as "I love to fondle your ----."

It was not easy for Mrs. R. She took the tapes home and listened to herself saying things that would have given her parents acute apoplexy. But she persisted, and after a few months her persistence paid off. Little by little she became less tense, and began to enjoy sex. She had her first orgasm during intercourse. It was not completely satisfying. She experienced all the physiological excitement, but somehow there was no emotional involvement. Her husband, however, telephoned me from the office the next day to marvel. It was like a second honeymoon, he said.

The real breakthrough followed soon after. It was so unexpected it almost frightened her—a feeling that was quickly replaced by sheer delight. The erstwhile frigid woman had suddenly become multi-orgasmic. She told me she had experienced five or six climaxes—she had lost track of the exact count—in rapid succession.

Mrs. R. was fortunate in that her problem was secondary frigidity, which behavior therapists can deal with successfully in 80 to 85 percent of the cases. Primary frigidity, however, which afflicts one out of every one hundred American women, responds to therapy only 20 percent of the time.

A woman who has never achieved an orgasm under any conditions is said to be suffering from primary frigidity. Research to date has not determined how much of this condition is due to physical, and how much to psychological, causes. In any event, treatment is usually difficult; but there is just enough chance for success to make any therapy worth trying.

From a patient's detailed description of the sexual discomfort involved in primary frigidity, it is often obvious that the cause is physical. Several of my patients, in describing their sexual responses, indicated a hypersensitive clitoris. When sexually excited, the clitoris became so sensitive that any stimulation caused pain and consequent withdrawal. A medical colleague examined these patients, confirmed the findings, and prescribed an ointment containing a mild anesthetic similar to that suggested for men with premature-ejaculation problems.

With two of the women involved, the anesthesia reduced the sensitivity just enough to eliminate the pain and allow them to achieve orgasm for the first time in their lives. I attempted to desensitize the other two to the feeling of pain, but without success.

Other methods exist for the treatment of primary frigidity, but so much research is still required in this area that I shall forgo describing them. I will say, however, that some methods used to treat secondary frigidity occasionally work in primary frigidity. One method in particular, involving guided imagery, will be discussed later in this chapter.

Most women who recoil from sex because it is painful to them are actually made frigid by *fear* of pain. They can therefore be treated in a manner effective for other phobias —by systematic desensitization, which has been discussed previously.

Vaginismus is often associated with frigidity. Here the vaginal muscles tighten up, not only making penetration painful or impossible, but also causing the muscle spasm itself to be painful even in the absence of sexual activity. The usual treatment is desensitization—through both imagery and actual life experience—to the introduction of slender objects into her vagina. The hierarchy is arranged so that the patient pictures objects increasing in diameter, starting with something as thin as a rectal thermometer. If there is tension when the patient first pictures inserting the thermometer, she is relaxed, and then presented with the image again and again until she can visualize it without tension.

The next step is for the patient actually to insert a thermometer at home. She does this over and over again as often as often as needed until she feels no tension during the act. After this step is completed, the husband inserts the thermometer into the vagina. Again this process is repeated until no tension is present.

A slightly larger object is used for the next phase of the therapy and the procedure is repeated. Dr. Wolpe reports that he has used wax candles of increasing diameters. Vaginal dilators, available at any surgical supply store, have also been used. Whatever the medium, the program is continued until an object at least the diameter of an average penis can be accommodated without tension and without painful vaginal contractions.·

As a final stage the husband introduces his well-lubricated penis into the wife's vagina a little at a time. No coital movements should be allowed until the entire penis can be accommodated. Patience and understanding are required of the husband; but they pay off.

Sometimes the fear of pain is not rationally founded (it is in women with vaginismus), even though there may have been a painful experience in the past. Mrs. D., for example, came to consult me because before marriage she had been ready and willing—even eager—for sex, and now she dreaded it. She had been married for several months and had not yet reached a sexual climax. Was she to be frigid all her life?

Mrs. D. was an attractive young college graduate. She enjoyed her job, was bright, alert, and, she had always thought, abreast of her generation. Before marriage she had not considered herself inhibited, only cautious. She had had no premarital intercourse, but she had indulged in heavy petting, which on occasion had advanced to the stage of mutual masturbation.

Her wedding night was a disaster. The bridegroom was as sexually inexperienced as he was frenzied in his ardor. There was no tenderness, no gentle consideration; the defloration was brutal. The bride's pain was intense, and, since her hymen was intact, there was blood shed. Mrs. D. was frightened as well as hurt.

Ever since that night she anticipated pain whenever her husband began undressing. She had also developed a real fear of physical injury. She remembered all the stories she had heard about the perils of unbridled copulation—girls bleeding to death after a sex orgy, vaginas torn and mutilated for life by husbands with overdeveloped genitalia.

She relaxed easily, pictured scenes vividly, and we had no trouble formulating a hierarchy. In the scenes with the least anxiety she pictured newspaper headlines: BRIDE HOSPITALIZED WITH MASSIVE HEMORRHAGE . . . HONEYMOON ENDS ON OPERATING TABLE; SEX MAIMS GIRL; TEN STITCHES NEEDED. . . . Eventually she was able to picture these, and then more personally graphic scenes at the top of the hierarchy, without tension. She became less tense during sex play.

Nevertheless, there was still such a strong anticipation of pain that she could not yet allow her husband to enter her. Further desensitization proved unsuccessful.

The method that overcame her last difficulty was similar to that used for vaginismus—with one difference. The therapeutic object had to be sexually stimulating because sexual feelings usually counteract anxiety. I sent her home with a vibrator, which she was instructed to use to stimulate her clitoris several times a day. After she began to enjoy the sensations produced by the vibrator, she was to insert it into her vagina a little more each day. As enjoyment gradually replaced dread, she was to let her husband take over and gently insert the vibrator. Only when she enjoyed this stage was sexual intercourse to be considered.

For their first attempts at coition, Mr. and Mrs. D. were instructed to adopt a reverse position—he should lie on his back so that she could lower herself slowly, allowing herself complete control and the ability to withdraw if she felt a return of the old fear.

After nearly eight months of desensitization she was no longer frigid. I made a follow-up phone call several months later. She told me they were having sex regularly —and enjoying every minute of it.

The desensitization technique that was so successful with Mrs. D. was of no use at all to Mrs. W., a down-to-earth businesswoman pushing fifty. Mrs. W. could not visualize. We had to find other means to recondition her.

Mrs. W. did not consider herself frigid. She had never refused herself to her husband. But after twenty-five years of marriage her husband had lost interest in her sexually and had begun to stray. What was she doing wrong?

Despite her hard-shelled exterior, she was genuinely fond of her husband. The prospect of lost security did not worry her; she could always take care of herself. But her husband was all she had to love now that their son was on his own, and she wanted her man to be happy.

Mr. W. readily confirmed his wife's suspicions. He had indeed been browsing in greener fields. He had only the kindliest feelings toward his wife, but after twenty-five years, going to bed with her was a great bore. His current frustration was not new. Now that he thought about it, she had always been "up tight about sex," he said.

Mrs. W.'s background was, as might be suspected,

puritanical. She regarded copulation as a marital duty to be performed as quickly as possible, with no fuss or feathers. Sex was restricted to intercourse; she wanted no foreplay, no preliminary fondling or exploratory caresses. Any but the orthodox face-to-face posture in intercourse was indecent. Masturbation was taboo. Oral sex was double taboo. So was sex during her menstrual periods. Her husband was right: she *was* up tight about sex.

When I discovered that Mrs. W. could not picture herself in the anxiety-provoking situations suggested by any imaginary list, I resorted to real pictures—vivid "pornographic" photographs. And when I say "pornographic," I do not mean the undraped nudes of cheap art magazines or *Playboy*'s center fold-out. I mean "feelthy peechers" like those that used to be peddled surreptitiously on Paris streets and are now legally obtainable in Scandinavia —photos of sexual activity so graphic that when I had them reproduced on slides, I had to accompany them with a letter certifying that they were to be used for therapeutic purposes.

The treatment made use of these slides in the implosive method. Implosion is like throwing a person afraid of water into the deep end of the pool. The patient is put into an intense-anxiety situation and is allowed to panic long enough for the panic to wear off and the fear to vanish. Rather than trust Mrs. W.'s subjective report, I hooked her up to a galvanic skin reflex indicator, one of the elements of the lie detector. The instrument records emotional reactions, measured by perspiration on the skin surface which reduces electrical resistance and causes a galvanometer needle to swing.

When I flashed the first slide, the galvanometer needle hit the top. Her whole body became rigid and her face froze. I instructed her to keep looking at the picture, to try to put herself into it, and to make up fantasies around it. The needle remained fixed at the edge of the scale for five minutes, ten minutes, twenty minutes. After almost half an hour the needle began to drop slowly back to zero, and I could see her body relax.

I let her relax and then flashed on the next slide. The same reaction occurred, but this time it didn't last quite so long.

The procedure was repeated for many sessions, with the panic constantly decreasing. During this period some interesting changes took place in her. Her facial expression became softer. She became more aware of men as men. She began to enjoy the physical sensations of her own body, even during such a simple act as walking. However, we were still far from our goal. Although much of the anxiety which was an obstacle to her freedom had been removed, she still had to be taught how to be free sexually. The lessons started with masturbation.

She was instructed to take warm baths instead of showers, and to enjoy the relaxation that came from just lying in the warm water. She was to allow herself to drift from relaxation to an erotic mood. She should discover her clitoris, stroke it, fondle it. Eventually she brought herself to climax, and she came to enjoy the experience thoroughly.

Training then went on to sex play with her husband. By this time she cooperated enthusiastically. And Mr. W., as he watched the changes taking place in his wife, abandoned his philandering to participate in her re-education. "She's a new woman," he told me as he took her home from her last session.

Part of Mrs. W.'s trouble was sheer ignorance; it is amazing how many other cases of frigidity in women are caused by the lack of sex education. Many people who should know better—including men, for too often a frigid woman can blame her mate's sexual ignorance for her condition—are woefully uninformed about the facts of life.

For example, many women who come to me do not understand the function or importance of the clitoris in sex relations. They are usually the same ones who are ignorant of the part foreplay has in achieving greater sexual satisfaction. Very often a simple lesson in anatomy or sexual techniques can restore a frigid woman to normalcy. Mrs. U. was such a case.

Mrs. U. was an attractive thirty-eight-year-old widow when she came to consult me. When she married at twenty-six, she had had no actual sex experience. Her husband died when she was thirty-two. They had had no children. She had been growing increasingly lonely during the intervening years, and she was anxious to remarry. Only the idea of sex put her off. She wanted a home and companionship. She had found a man who wanted to marry her, and whom she was fond of, but the idea of sleeping with him—with anyone, in fact—was so odious to her that it outweighed the advantages of marriage. Was she really frigid?

We went into the history of her marriage. Although it had not been completely arid sexually, neither had it been terribly satisfying. In all six years of marriage she had achieved orgasm only three or four times. Her husband had apparently been sexually inexperienced and completely self-centered. He thought only of his own satisfaction—the bam-bam-thank-you-ma'am type. There had never been any foreplay. Either he was bored by it, or he was not aware of how important the tender and increasingly exciting preliminaries can be, particularly for a woman, to mutually successful sexual intercourse. He had usually ejaculated before she was even properly lubricated.

Mrs. U. had experimented with sex a few times since her husband's death, always with unhappy results. Apparently she had learned from her experience with her husband that the sex act was limited to minimal foreplay and rapid entry, with no concern for her own satisfaction. She probably encouraged other men to act accordingly. The whole business of copulation became distasteful—something to be avoided. She wasn't sure she wanted to marry her current suitor if she was going to have to put up with sex on demand for the rest of her life.

I explained to her what she should have learned from her late husband: that while men are usually ready for coitus almost at the drop of a pair of panties, women have to be led up to the critical moment by successive stages; that before the right responses have been triggered, and the secretions necessary to her full enjoyment of sex released, at least twenty minutes must usually elapse. I told her that if her sex hangup were the only thing that stood in the way of remarriage, she should put her current suitor to the test. The next time he wants to make love to you, I said, see that you get your quota of preliminary loving before the actual sex act. Don't let him in until there has been at least half an hour of foreplay.

"To be certain you don't fall back into your old habits, use a kitchen timer. Set it for half an hour, and no intercourse until the bell rings." She followed our plan and reported to me that to her surprise she had actually enjoyed the act. A week later she achieved orgasm.

Mrs. U.'s problem of "frigidity" was solved by simply applying what should be common knowledge.

Widespread myths about what is proper or improper in sex are responsible for much of what seems to be frigidity. Different women find some positions in coitus more stimulating than others, but like Mrs. W., they are reluctant to adopt any but the papa-mama posture for fear of seeming indecent. Many quite normal practices are widely regarded as depraved. The importance and the techniques of foreplay are too extensively unknown, as Mrs. U. discovered and as too many unhappy women have yet to discover. Too few unsatisfied wives consult their family physician or a marriage counselor.

When patients come to me with an inadequate or mistaken knowledge of anatomy and physiology, I first refer them to standard works on the subject of sex, books like Albert Ellis's *The Art and Science of Sex,* or *The Sexually Responsive Woman* by Drs. Eberhard and Phyllis Kronhausen. A number of marriage manuals now available contain photographs illustrating foreplay and various coital positions.

One type of specialized sex education called guided imagery is an outgrowth of a technique devised by Wolpin and Rachman. I have used it successfully in treating both women who have never experienced an orgasm and women who, because of some emotional block or for lack of a partner, have gone so many years without a climax that they have forgotten what it is like. The tool I use for teaching them is a modeling tape.

With the cooperation of an articulate young woman who has no sexual hangups, I prepared a tape recording which describes the bodily sensations and mounting emotional excitement of a sexual experience from the first kiss through orgasm to the postcoital calm. Her seductive voice carries the listener along as the preliminary titillation grows to a tingling warmth that spreads through the body to explode in ecstasy.

Since different women respond differently, it is often a good idea to tailor a special similar tape to fit the individual patient. One woman who had gone three years without a climax said: "No, no. I remember now. That's not the way I felt." So together we worked up a new script, which I taped in my voice because she found that reading it in her own voice produced too much anxiety.

The patient follows a regular procedure with the tape,

first in my office, later in her home. She begins by putting herself into a state of deep relaxation; then she listens to the tape, then relaxes again. Specific parts of the tape that have caused tension may be used as scenes for desensitization. If she can picture herself actually experiencing the taped reactions, perhaps she will eventually come to do it in real life.

A few women have been depressed by listening to the tape, because they have never experienced the feelings it described. Most, however, find that it helps restructure their thinking about sex and heightens sexual pleasure, even if they still do not reach climax. Some have been helped to achieve orgasm.

The woman takes the tape home with her and, while relaxed, plays it three or four times a day for five or six weeks. If she then becomes bored by it, and her mind wanders, we either cut a new tape to measure or change our approach.

Despite the special cases mentioned, the greatest cause of sexual inadequacy still appears to be anxiety or fear, and relaxation or desensitization is usually the treatment of choice. Lazarus, formerly of Temple University Medical School and now at Yale, has used the method in group therapy, treating four women at a time and achieving 75 percent success. The "hierarchy"—the succession of imaginary anxiety-provoking scenes presented to the patient in deep relaxation—is approximately the same in group as in individual therapy. It proceeds from mild to greater tension as follows:

> Embracing
> Kissing
> Petting while clothed
> Undressing
> Mutual fondling in the nude

> Perception of husband's erect penis
> Penetration
> Shift in position during copulation

When the patient signals that she feels tension, the series stops until she is relaxed again.

Just as physical exercises have been devised for men with sexual difficulties, others are available for women who have trouble achieving orgasm. Some are described in *Human Sexual Inadequacy* by Masters and Johnson.

The indispensable role of a sympathetic, understanding, and patient husband cannot be stressed too much. A good man is just as important in helping a woman with her sex problems as a good woman is in rescuing a man. The basic rules remain the same. Keep tension low, sexual stimulation high. Do not press for a climax, just let it come.

While systematic desensitization is usually effective when frigidity is the result of fears—fear of pregnancy, fear of pain, fear of not achieving an orgasm—this is not the only tension-reduction method at our disposal. Aversion relief is another such method. This technique, described in Chapter 6, is based on the idea that the removal of an unpleasant stimulus is a positive reinforcement. It is sometimes used for the elimination of fears connected with frigidity.

Mrs. R. was turned off by men in general, yet she was by no means homosexual. We were able to narrow her fear down to a particular object: the penis. The aversion relief in her case consisted in seating her beside a desk covered with photographs of naked men and detailed enlargements of penises in various stages of readiness. I then attached to her arms the electrodes leading to the secondary circuit of an induction coil which when turned on would give her an unpleasant but not dangerous electric shock.

Initially, she sat beside the desk looking at her lap, the

walls, anything but the pictures. During this time she received a continuous electric shock. When she could stand the shock no longer, she turned to look at the photographs of penises. The moment she looked, the shock stopped. The positive reinforcement of relief from the painful stimulus became associated with the male genitalia. After a number of sessions the fear diminished and her frigidity disappeared.

Sexual problems of women, like those of men, may sometimes result from lack of assertion. In these cases frigidity is treated by assertive training. If a woman feels that she cannot say "no" when her husband is thinking "yes," she may yield with an unexpressed reluctance that is hardly conducive to complete sexual fulfillment. Reluctance becomes resentment and resentment builds to anger. The wife feels abused and put upon. Her resentment is transferred to the sex act, and she becomes tense—and frigid.

To unfreeze her, the first step is to teach her how to say no.

One of my frigid patients was helped by the assertive method, even though her tension was not directly connected with sex. Mrs. T. was a young housewife with three small children. She came from a lower-middle-class Jewish family. Her husband was an accountant who often brought tax work home at night to help make ends meet. Mrs. T. suffered from chronic depression, which in itself tends to cripple the sex drive. On the rare occasions when she experienced an orgasm, she and her husband were on vacation—away from home.

It soon became obvious that her problem was lack of assertion. She was being pushed around by her children and by her mother, who fit the image of the stereotypical Jewish mother to a T.

Mama was constantly on the phone, worrying about

something. "You sound tired. . . . Are you feeling all right? . . . Maybe I should come right over. . . . Is that Sarah I hear coughing still? . . . Did you give her some onion syrup like I told you? . . . Listen, I'm going downtown this afternoon shopping. I want you should come with me. . . ."

Mrs. T. couldn't say no to her three children either. She was stern with them when they interfered with her housework, but when she sat down to rest, read the newspaper, or watch a television program of her own choosing, they were upon her en masse, competing for attention. Although she was the martyr type who outwardly gloried in how much she did for her children and how much she put herself out to please her mother, she actually resented the subservient role thrust upon her, and a growing tenseness was the result.

First I tried relaxation on Mrs. T., but after a session or two I saw that it would not work. I turned to the assertive technique. Together we devised what she assured me were typical scenes with her mother and her children. I supplied the dialogue I thought she needed. In a phone conversation with her mother, she was to say, "No, Mama, don't come over today. I'll see you day after tomorrow, as we planned." And to her children: "Can't you see that I'm reading the newspaper? Go play quietly until I've finished."

I made tape recordings of these scenes. She took them home, so she could listen to herself saying *no* in her own voice.

Little by little she found elbow room in her own life. Her sexual problem, which was part of her general lack of assertion, resolved itself when she felt she had more control over her life again. She resumed playing the piano, an activity she had neglected since the birth of her second child. She also took up tennis for the first time since the first year of her marriage. The T. household, her husband told me, had become a much more pleasant place, thanks to Mrs. T.'s new, assertive behavior.

The assertive training techniques, which served Mrs. T. so successfully, are discussed in detail (as applied to fields other than sex) in Chapter 4.

Although many men consult a behavior therapist because of problems of deviation and other unusual manifestations of sex, few women seek treatment for this type of problem. Most sexual problems of women involve some degree of frigidity, but I do see some cases of promiscuity.

Interestingly enough, promiscuity very often has little direct connection with sex. Let me illustrate by describing three promiscuous patients whom I was able to help through behavior therapy methods.

1) Lydia was a rather shy, good-looking college girl of twenty. Although she was very intelligent and received good marks, she seemed to wallow in self-disparagement. She had a domineering father and a retiring mother, from whom she had apparently learned unassertive behavior. Her inability to say no extended to her sexual behavior as well. She would go to bed with almost any man who asked her, without any strong feelings, pro or con. Eventually she began going to bed with men she actually disliked. She hated herself for it afterward, but seemed unable to stop. At this point she came to me for help.

Although Lydia's trouble was quite different from Mrs. T.'s, the basic cause was the same: she couldn't say no. And the therapy was the same: assertive training. We reviewed scenes from her past experiences, discussed them, and worked out responses she could have made—responses that would have helped her avoid many predicaments.

The program was, in a sense, laboratory preparation for practical application—dialogue rehearsal, anticipation of situations she might have to meet, evaluation of her options. She applied what she had learned to new situations or repetitions of old ones. When she came back we discussed what had caused her successes and her failures. Assertive training gradually helped Lydia master her social life. She developed discrimination concerning men, and her self-esteem rose immeasurably. Quite simply, she regained the power of choice.

2) Annette came to consult me because she was distressed by the loss of her self-respect. She did not enjoy being promiscuous, but it was a compulsion she did not know how to cope with. The root of her trouble, as in many cases of promiscuity, was a phobia; in her case, two phobias. She was afraid of being alone, and tried to counter the fear by being with a different man every night. She also dreaded not being liked. She was afraid that if she said no, the man would be furious and broadcast unkind things about her, with the result that she would lose all her friends and be lonelier than ever.

The first step in Annette's therapy was to persuade her to get a roommate. The second was to desensitize her to the fear of being unpopular and alone. This was done by relaxing her, and then presenting a series of imaginary situations, all increasingly anxiety-provoking, beginning with her overhearing two girls whispering about her and ending with her being publicly ostracized at a ball attended by all her friends and relatives. When her fears were dispelled, her promiscuity stopped.

3) Virginia's promiscuity was a cover for her fear of forming close personal relationships. She had been badly hurt in her first love affair, and she was determined not to let it happen again. To avoid becoming emotionally involved with any one man, she wandered from bed to bed, congratulating herself on being free of regrets, commitments, or future heartaches. Then Virginia began to wake up in the morning with a hangover of self-doubt. What

was she doing to herself? Did she have the freedom she wanted, or had she made herself a slave to something she really didn't want? At this point she came to see me.

After assaying her background and personality, I came to the conclusion that Virginia's open-door policy in sexual relations was phobic in origin. She was dubious at first, but she collaborated with me in preparing a hierarchy, listing her fears in the reverse order of their anxiety potential.

Virginia's fear of closeness was based on the fear of being hurt. The hierarchy consisted of different men saying various unpleasant things to her. The scene lowest in anxiety content was a total stranger looking at her, an expression of mild contempt on his face. At the top of the hierarchy she was to picture an imaginary husband whom she loved dearly telling her that he hated her because she was a terrible person. Twenty-two intervening steps filled in the hierarchy.

Virginia responded readily to relaxation and sytematic desensitization. She lost her fear of falling in love, and the last I heard she was at the point of forsaking all others.

One unusual case was that of a formerly promiscuous woman who became frigid upon marrying the love of her life. Betty B. had been an airline stewardess. When she first came to see me she was an attractive woman approaching thirty and had been married recently. She enjoyed sex and had indulged herself rather freely, even before the advent of the pill. In fact, she had undergone one abortion. She had smoked pot socially and experimented with amphetamines and other drugs, including LSD, but she was by no means an addict. She was merely conforming to the mores of her generation.

She and her husband had been sleeping together for some time before their marriage; the moment they were married, however, Betty became up tight about sex. She and her husband had enjoyed a completely uninhibited relationship before the wedding, but since then she had been unable to reach a climax. What was wrong?

During our diagnostic conversation I found that her problem resulted from two sources of tension. First, she had guilt feelings about her free-wheeling past, her abortion, and her experimentation with drugs. Second, she wanted children, but was afraid that her past excesses might cause her children to be born deformed.

The therapy was systematic desensitization with hierarchies on two separate levels—one to deal with her need for the self-denunciation that caused her unhappy tensions, and the other to get rid of the phobia about bearing a deformed child. She responded to both.

For the sexually disturbed woman who seeks help, behavior therapy has much to offer. With problems ranging from frigidity to promiscuity, its methods have produced a long series of successes. There have been failures, too, for there is no magic involved. But on the whole the techniques of behavior therapy do provide means for rearranging the unsatisfactory sex lives of troubled women.

9

PROBLEM CHILDREN DON'T HAVE TO
GROW UP TO BE ADULTS WITH PROBLEMS

PROBLEM CHILDREN react very well to conditioned-reflex treatment. Since behavior-therapy theory is based on the learning process, the ideal time to modify individual behavior is before the individual has learned to do too many things wrong. The same principles applied to help disturbed adults are useful in defusing many difficulties of children, from the baby's temper tantrums through the disruptiveness of the hyperactive schoolchild to the adolescent's hostility toward his elders.

There is one big difference, however, between treating adults and treating children. The parents are often a part of their children's problems. Children are not *born* to misbehave. They *learn* to do things considered "bad." They learn to fight with their siblings or friends, to refuse to eat, to be frightened of other people. If they learn these things, somebody must be teaching them, and this somebody is usually the parents. Without being aware of it, parents often reinforce the behavior they complain about, and fail to reinforce the behavior they want.

For example, a mother complains that her child is so noisy that he is driving her crazy. She has to yell at him constantly to keep him quiet. Let's examine this situation for cause and effect.

When the child is playing quietly, the mother goes about her daily routine and ignores him. The child gets no reinforcement for playing quietly, so this behavior is weakened and is less likely to be repeated.

When the child becomes noisy enough, his mother comes in to yell at him and the child is quiet for a while. There are two consequences to this pair of reactions. 1) The yelling, although it may be unpleasant, still represents attention for the child from his mother. The yelling is positive reinforcement; the child's noisy behavior is encouraged and will be repeated. The mother is actually training her child to be noisy. 2) The child has (temporarily) become quiet—positive reinforcement for his mother's yelling behavior. Consequently she is likely to yell more often. In other words, the child is actually training his mother to yell.

Both are caught in a vicious circle. The mother goes on training the child to be noisy and the child keeps training his mother to yell.

How do we break the circle? Obviously the trick is to reinforce the desired behavior and stop reinforcing that which is objectionable. The mother should pay attention to her child when he is playing quietly and ignore him when he is noisy. This should increase the frequency of his calmer moments and decrease his noisy play.

If the noise becomes too much, the mother may use a "time-out" procedure. She may remove the child from all positive reinforcement by putting him in a room where there are no toys or other pleasant distractions. Left there for five minutes, the child soon learns that noise does not pay.

The results of this method are neither magical nor immediate. They require time and patience on the part of the mother. Preparing such a program involves technicalities, too. An excellent and easily understood book on the subject, *Living with Children,* by Patterson and Gullion, is listed in the bibliography.

It is frequently necessary to condition the mother or father in order for psychotherapy to be effective with the child.

A classic case study was reported in 1959 by C. D. Williams in the *Journal of Abnormal and Social Psychology*. The experimenter eliminated tantrum behavior in a twenty-one-month-old infant who invariably cried unless one of his parents stayed with him until he fell asleep. The treatment was simple. The parents were told to ignore the tantrum and leave the crying child, closing the door to his room as they left. On first trial, the crying lasted for forty-five minutes. On subsequent nights, however, the tantrums followed the standard "extinction curve" downward until the crying stopped completely after ten nights. There were no abnormal side effects and a follow-up some months later found the child normal and quite friendly.

It is understandable for parents to grow tense after listening to a baby crying for forty-five minutes, and they frequently need guidance, if not therapy. They must be warned that withdrawal of reinforcement may cause an initial increase in the tantrums. The child may feel that the crying that brought him attention in the past was no longer working because he was not being violent enough. The "extinction curve" may therefore rise somewhat before it starts downward.

Parents may sometimes be helped to stop reinforcing undesired behavior by changing their reaction to it. Just desensitizing the mother may change the child. One mother I treated was a graduate student working for her Ph.D. She was married and had a baby whose crying disturbed her studying. When the baby cried she became anxious, so it seemed that she was always running in to see if the crying had been caused by an open safety pin, a touch of colic, or a need to be burped. After the interruption she had trouble getting back to her books. I told her the crying would probably stop if she stopped reinforcing the baby's behavior. She replied that she couldn't bear to hear the baby carrying on like that, even though trying to make him stop upset her too.

I devoted a session to desensitizing her to the sound of crying, and she went home after having listened in imagination to repeated crying spells with diminishing anxiety. She returned a week later to announce that she was able to study without interruption because she had discovered that the disturbing sounds were not really crying, but were pleasant noises like cooing and gurgling. By lowering her anxiety, that one session had changed her perception of the child's crying.

Another woman complained that her young son upset her by making grotesque faces all day long. She had tried to make him stop by scolding him, yelling at him, even spanking him once for laughing when she told him that if he continued, his face would be permanently distorted. His behavior did not change, obviously because it gained his mother's attention.

She and I drew up a simple hierarchy of three or four scenes picturing young Bobby's clowning for attention. They made her tense at first, but by the end of the session most of her anxiety was gone. When she went home, I was satisfied that she would probably be able to ignore her son's grimaces without tension. Seven weeks later she announced: "Yesterday my husband remarked to me that Bobby had stopped making those faces. I paid so little attention to them that I didn't even notice when they stopped."

Sometimes a combination of positive reinforcement with the withdrawal of reinforcement has been found useful in modifying the disruptive behavior of children in a classroom. Dr. Gerald R. Patterson, 1971–72 president of the Association for the Advancement of Behavior Therapy, applied such methods in the case of a hyperactive nine-year-old boy. His teacher had been cautioned against reinforcing his behavior by giving him the attention he wanted, but she found it difficult to deal with his classmates, who were enormously entertained by his antics and encouraged him by their laughter. Dr. Patterson suggested the use of a "magic teaching machine" which dispensed pennies and candy to both the boy and his audience as rewards for fixed periods of undivided attention. The reward brought a withdrawal of reinforcement by the other pupils almost immediately, and within four weeks the boy's behavior had normalized.

Dr. Dorothy J. Suskind of New York City's Hunter College conducted a significant experiment in handling disruptive classroom behavior in 1969. She assembled fourth-to sixth-grade teachers from ghetto schools and divided them into two groups. One group studied the classroom problems cold. The other was given group therapy consisting of relaxation and systematic desensitization. The hierarchy devised for the latter group consisted of scenes of their pupils jumping up, running around the classroom, fighting, and throwing things.

The follow-up was made by a supervisor who did not know which teachers had been desensitized and which had taken the course without therapy. His evaluation showed that the desensitized teachers were much better able to cope with the actual classroom situation. They had developed no more liking for undisciplined hell-raising, but they could face it without tension or anxiety. And they were able to handle a disruptive situation calmly, rationally, and without panic.

Sometimes unruly behavior exceeds toleration. Instead of ordering the ringleader to stand in a corner, a teacher who has learned something about behavior-therapy methods now takes him to a quiet room isolated from the reinforcing approval of his classmates. She leaves him there for ten or fifteen minutes before returning him to a calmer classroom.

School phobias—an anxiety reaction that results in persistent absence from classes—are not uncommon among children. Two causes seem to be at the root of this problem.

The first is fear of separation from parents. The child responds to the prospect of going to school by absolute refusal, or by inventing an excuse—a stomach ache, for instance—to stay home. Usually he can count on support by someone in the family.

The second is fear of some specific object or situation in the school itself—strangeness in entering a new school, anxiety about having to recite, reprimand by the teacher, rejection by his classmates.

Treatment for both types of school phobia is the same as treatment for adult phobias: to accustom the child to the situation *without* anxiety by some graduated form of desensitization. If it is fear of separation, the mother accompanies the child to school at first, and little by little moves outside the classroom and finally outside the schoolhouse. At each step away from mother, the child receives positive reinforcement.

Dr. Patterson had a case of this sort[*] referred to him by a school nurse. The subject was seven-year-old Carl, a first-grade pupil who in the second week of the term would not stay in school unless one of his parents stayed with him. He had shown the same insecurity elsewhere. He played only in the immediate vicinity of his home, and even then interrupted his play frequently to enter the house to see if his mother was still there. If Mama went shopping, Carl had to go along.

In school he had a low reading score but a high IQ. He

[*] Ullman and Krasner, *Case Studies in Behavior Modification.*

was an attractive child, but seemed immature for his age. He had a serious articulation defect, which may have contributed to the fact that neither coaxing nor threats of punishment would keep him in school.

Carl was terrified when his mother took him to the Patterson clinic. The therapists decided to try a combination of positive reinforcement with a modeling technique as pioneered by Bandura—a role-playing procedure in which Carl did the thinking for a doll character named Henry, who was Carl's age. Positive reinforcement was one M&M candy.

Carl's mama remained in the playroom for the first session, and Carl got one M&M whenever thirty seconds elapsed without his looking at his mother. At the second session, he agreed to let Mama sit outside the playroom with the door closed. For this he was rewarded with two M&Ms.

Meanwhile the therapist let Carl guide Henry through visits to a doctor, the school, and a playground. Since Carl was afraid of playing with bigger boys, the therapist prompted him to let Henry join a rough game in which he scraped his knee. When Carl agreed that Henry should put a Band-Aid on his leg himself instead of running to his mother, he got an extra M&M.

Carl's parents were encouraged to give him social reinforcement at home. When Carl stayed outside for a whole hour without entering the house to reassure himself that Mama was still there, his mother announced the fact to the family at dinner, and his father praised him for his bravery.

When Carl went back to school, he was accompanied for the first few days by a tutor who had been keeping him abreast of his class studies. On the fifth day Carl announced he was no longer afraid to go to school alone. As Dr. Patterson concludes: "After twenty bags of M&Ms and ten hours of staff work, Carl returned to school."

With the operant method of changing children's conduct, rewards must be contingent upon performance of the desired behavior. This point may be illustrated by the program I devised for a woman patient whose children went off to school in the morning, leaving their room in a mess. No amount of scolding or coaxing had any effect. I suggested that the mother make breakfast contingent upon the neatness of their room.

Mrs. R. was shocked by the idea of her youngsters' going without breakfast. I assured her that missing a meal or two would not hurt two healthy girls, aged seven and nine, and that eating was often used as a form of reinforcement in psychotherapy.

When Mrs. R. agreed to try my proposed plan of action, I told her she had to specifically define the behavior she wanted from her children. For our purposes they were to meet four criteria: *All* dirty clothes in the hamper. *No* clothes on the floor. Beds made. *All* toys and games off the floor and either in the toy box or on the shelf. I had to desensitize her to the idea of acting the part of the Wicked Witch of the West, but she went through with it.

She explained the rules to the girls that night, and inspected the room after they had come downstairs next morning. It was still a mess. The room was not satisfactory, she told them, so there would be no breakfast.

The announcement met with loud protests and even tears, but Mrs. R. stood her ground. "You didn't meet the conditions. No breakfast. Hurry or you'll miss the school bus." She ignored further protests.

Next morning the room was a little neater, but there were dirty clothes on the floor. Again no breakfast was served.

The third morning the room passed inspection and the girls ate breakfast. Occasional relapses occurred, but if mother turned thumbs down, the girls went back and cleaned up the room.

If the girls had been old enough to challenge the rules with a "Don't kids have any rights?" the answer might have been the words of Dr. Richard Stewart of the University of Michigan: Rights have to be earned.

Although enuresis—incontinence of urine—is sometimes an adult problem, we are interested here in its relation to children. Behavior therapists have become seriously concerned with the problem of bed-wetting—as it is more simply called—and have done a considerable amount of experimental and clinical investigation in the area.

Enuresis is caused by tension in the bladder, which in turn causes urination without waking the child. In treating the problem, we try by using the bladder tension to condition the child to wake up so that he can get to the bathroom before he wets the bed.

The device used is a simple one, consisting of two layers of copper gauze imbedded in a cotton pad. The copper gauze is connected to a battery, a very sensitive relay, and an electric bell. The child sleeps on top of this pad.

As urine has electrolytic properties, the first drops start the current flowing between the layers of copper gauze. The relay is activated and the bell rings, awakening the child, who should have time to contract his sphincter voluntarily, get out of bed, and go to the toilet. In this way waking behavior is conditioned to bladder tension and eventually he will awake before the bell rings and get to the bathroom before he starts wetting. Finally he will not wake up at all and sleep through the night—dry. At no time does the child get a shock.

Simple as the procedure seems, it has pitfalls, the most serious of which involves parental cooperation. Parents become co-therapists in the treatment of enuresis, and it is often difficult for them to understand what they are supposed to do and to do it properly. Sometimes the child himself will disconnect the battery so that the bell will not ring. Sometimes defects appear spontaneously, as they will in any electrical apparatus. All these possibilities must be ruled out, however, before the method can be called a failure. The pad-and-bell apparatus is generally obtainable in the United States. The Sears, Roebuck stores sell it.

Modifications of this method have been found to be equally effective. In general the various studies report from 53 to 100 percent cures. The lower figure, however, may be misleading and may reflect the lack of professional control over the procedure. Longer follow-ups show that there is some relapse rate among the bed-wetters, but 45 percent of the backsliders respond to retraining. There is certainly need for more experimentation in the field of enuresis.

There seems to be no evidence of symptom substitution among those successfully treated. The children have not shown personality disturbance or other symptoms after they have stopped bed-wetting; on the whole they seem happier and better adjusted.

The treatment of mentally retarded children has been revolutionized during the last six to eight years through the application of behavior-therapy techniques. Columbus (Ohio) State Institution, for instance, in assessing potential rehabilitation of the retarded, has moved away from traditional measurements of intellectual and social maturity to a behavior checklist. The list is broken down into behavioral components and becomes virtually a program for therapy.

The operant methods have been found the most useful. A system of rewards helps the most severely retarded children learn the essential self-help skills—walking, eating, personal hygiene, toilet use. A program is tailored for each child, undesirable behavior slated for extinction is ignored, desirable behavior is positively reinforced by approving words and candy or its equivalent. There is no reason to believe that a retarded child, even one with severe brain damage, cannot be taught, given the proper conditions.

Less seriously retarded children are taught the social skills most successfully in institutions where a token economy translates the operant techniques into everyday practices. Retarded girls learn dressing and undressing, cleanliness, grooming, and other basics in return for tokens —the reinforcers—with which they can buy treats and special privileges. Token fines are also imposed for inappropriate behavior. The reinforcement techniques are making it possible for many of these girls to return to the community.

Operant techniques are also being used in teaching autistic children to talk. Correctly imitating a sound—*yes, no,* or *maybe*—merits a reward. Some success has been reported, although critics have questioned whether imitating sounds will lead to true speech. Experimental work is proceeding in this field; much more is needed, however, before the evidence gathered can be called conclusive.

Aversive techniques are sometimes used for disturbed children, especially those showing compulsive behavior. An unusual case of compulsive arson was reported to the 1970 meeting of the Association for the Advancement of Behavior Therapy, by Dr. M. S. "Mickey" Denholtz of New York Medical College. The patient was a retarded seventeen-year-old schizophrenic boy. He occasionally fell down and lost consciousness, but there seemed to be nothing wrong with his central nervous system. Although he had been setting trash fires in the back yard and the basement for some time, his family did not become seriously concerned until their home caught fire in the small morning hours. The family members escaped injury, but the house burned to the ground.

The boy at first denied, then admitted, setting the blaze. He had heard voices telling him to do it. Voices always told him to set fires. When he was asked whether he would do it again, he said he would if the voices told him he should.

Dr. Denholtz and his crew prepared a series of photos of the boy lighting matches, setting fires, watching the flames. They also photographed him with his family smiling at him, sitting in the family car which he loved, and in other pleasant situations to be used as a relief series in the carrousel tray of a slide projector. The family—father, mother, sister, and brother—was enlisted to participate in the daily therapy started by Dr. Denholtz.

The patient could operate the projector, but the therapist controlled the electric apparatus, which gave the boy a strong shock when the incendiary slides were shown. The shock was stopped when the picture was changed to a pleasant family scene. For forty-five days the boy had daily sessions of fifteen minutes each. The number of sessions was then reduced to three a week, next to one a month. Finally they were discontinued altogether.

After the fifth week, the boy realized that the voices ordering him to set fires were imaginary. Midway in his therapy he testified to the effectiveness of the reconditioning: when he was told to strike a match, he could "feel" the electric shock even though he was not connected to the apparatus.

At the time of Dr. Denholtz's report, the boy was taking swimming lessons, learning judo, and working in a gas station, an unusual job for a former compulsive arsonist. His reconditioning had been so thorough, however, that he was unable to use the vulcanizer to repair inner tubes because he could not light a match. Dr. Denholtz gave him special training that would allow him to make an exception for the tire job.

Although the boy is still schizophrenic, there has been a great improvement in his life pattern, and the fire-setting behavior seems to be a thing of the past.

Shock therapy has been dramatically successful in treating seriously disturbed children. Drs. Bradley Boucher and Ivar Lovaas, while with the University of California at Los Angeles Hospital, described the case of a retarded seven-year-old boy who had had a self-destructive compulsion since the age of two, and had to be kept in complete restraint. When not wearing his camisole he would scream and beat his head against any nearby object. He could not be controlled with drugs, and his wild behavior was demoralizing to the hospital staff and dangerous to himself.

First the psychotherapists tried the extinction method of ignoring the child. Daily for eight days they gave the boy an hour and a half of freedom from restraint. Released from his straitjacket, he behaved as usual—apparently trying to kill himself. During the first days the therapists counted three thousand self-inflicted wounds, mostly about his head and ears. Over the entire eight-day period he accumulated ten thousand cuts and bruises. However, he took a careful aim and although the injuries were bloody and spectacular, they were far from fatal. On the last day of this experimental period, he struck himself only fifteen times. Then the aversive therapy was begun. Every time he hit his head he received a strong electric shock to his leg.

On the day the shocks were applied the hits stopped after the first one brought on aversion. In two weeks there was no more self-destructive behavior, even though the shocks were discontinued. The boy was taken home, where his behavior became that of a normal child. He gave no sign of his previous tendencies.

Operant conditioning is used to modify the behavior of adolescents as well as young children, although the character of the positive reinforcement must of course be different. Instead of candy or toys, the older youngsters are rewarded with theater tickets, mid-field seats for a football game, or the use of the family car on Saturday nights. (Social reinforcers—smiles, approving nods—are important at all ages.) Whatever most interests the child can usually be assumed to be potentially a positive reinforcement. The conditions for granting or withholding it should be spelled out precisely.

One of my patients was worried about his seventeen-year-old son, who he feared was well on the road to juvenile delinquency. The boy would stay out most of the night without telling his parents where he had been. His parents often stayed awake until three, four, or even five o'clock in the morning, waiting for him. The reinforcer to be used—the privilege he valued most—was the use of the family car on Saturday nights.

I suggested that the use of the car be made contingent on his getting home at a certain time every night. It was not precise enough to tell the boy he must be home early. The time must be fixed by mutual agreement, say 1 A.M. Then the parents could go to bed at their usual hour and set the alarm for one o'clock. When the alarm sounded, one of them could get up and check the boy's room. Whether he was home or not, the parents could then sleep until morning, when they could tell the son whether or not he had scored points toward his transportation for Saturday night.

He failed to meet the conditions for the first two Saturdays. After that he made the one o'clock deadline.

As I remarked at the beginning of this chapter, it is often necessary for a behavior therapist to treat the parents in order to influence the child. This holds true for the adolescent as well as for the toddler and the grade-school pupil.

A woman patient of mine came in one day in a state of great distress. Her son had come home from college on vacation and she and her husband were very much upset by the length of his hair. Her husband could talk of nothing else. "When are you getting your hair cut, Max?" he would say to his son. "Why can't you have short hair like decent people?" Both parents were concerned about his problems and progress at college. They wanted to ask him if he was still having trouble with trigonometry, if any of his friends were taking drugs, whether he had straightened out things with his draft board. His long hair, however, disrupted all communication between them.

I tried explaining to the mother that hair styles had nothing to do with character. She replied that she knew all about George Washington and Benjamin Franklin and their generation but she was still terribly disturbed by that rat's nest her son was so proud of. So I desensitized her to a few simple scenes involving the boy's long hair. I asked her to picture her long-haired son walking in while she was entertaining her bridge club, or visiting his father's office during a conference with the ultraconservative president of the firm. After much repetition she managed the visualization without tension.

Once the anxiety was gone, even though she still didn't like the long hair, she was able to re-establish communications with the boy. She also persuaded her husband to accept their son without losing his temper. They were then able to talk calmly about matters that were really important.

Once the pressure was off, the lad compromised a little. He didn't go so far as to have a crew cut, but he did have his hair trimmed somewhat, and even combed it neatly. The moment his parents had stopped fighting him, he stopped fighting back. Removing the tension by no means closed the generation gap, but it did permit constructive dialogue.

With the degree of control that can be exercised over the environment where children of all ages are involved, the operant methods are extremely powerful. Sometimes rather complex programs must be devised to establish or extinguish a given behavior pattern. Results are often a long time in coming. With care, patience, and the systematic and skillful use of reinforcers, however, behavioral changes can be brought about, even in young rebels. If no change takes place, something is usually wrong with the program, not the child, and a modified plan may lead in the desired direction.

10

PSYCHOLOGICAL "COMMON COLDS":

Learning to Deal with Stuttering, Overweight, Sexual Hangups, Hypochondria

MOST OF THE previous chapters have been devoted to explaining the methods and techniques of behavior therapy and to illustrating by case histories how they are applied to specific problems. In this chapter I would like to describe some of the more common problems the therapist is likely to encounter—obesity, stuttering, hypochondria, psychogenic ulcers, shyness—and how he chooses the appropriate technique to solve them. Let's start with the patient who stutters.

Many theories have been advanced about what causes stuttering. These range from neurological imbalance of the brain hemispheres, the presence of inhibitory forces, and deeply rooted personality conflicts, to the existence of anxiety, either general or specifically restricted to fear of stuttering. There is some evidence favoring each viewpoint, but there is also much evidence against all. At present we do not know the real cause of stuttering.

What we do know about the conditions that influence stuttering is applied in treating a stutterer through behavior therapy. It proved quite effective in the case of Mrs. Susan J.

Mrs. J. was a young housewife of twenty-eight, brought up in New York City, the second of three children born to college-educated middle-class parents. She had been a bright child, did well in school, and graduated from one of New York City's colleges. She was happily married to a professional man who treated her with understanding and consideration.

Her speech handicap did not circumscribe her social life, although she found it difficult to meet strangers. She had taken several years of speech therapy without result. Another two years of psychoanalysis had been equally unsuccessful. By the time she was nineteen, she had given up seeking a cure, and was resigned to stuttering for the rest of her life.

Why, then, did she come to me nine years later? Her three-and-a-half-year-old daughter was beginning to stutter, and in desperation she decided to see if behavior therapy could help.

Mrs. J. was an aggravated case of stuttering. When I asked her to read from a magazine, she stumbled two or three times in every sentence. The words came out explosively and with great effort, accompanied by grimaces and facial contortions. Her whole body seemed involved in the process of speaking, her muscles tensing convulsively when she faltered. I tape-recorded her reading so that we would have a basis to work from.

I explained that while we still did not know what caused her trouble, we did have certain empirical methods for treating it. One of these was rhythmic speech—if she could learn to speak to a certain fixed rhythm she might overcome her stutter. Mrs. J. understood this very well; she was an amateur singer, and had found that her stutter disappeared while she was singing, except when she was not sure of the lyrics.

I brought out a metronome, a simple instrument music teachers use, and set it for sixty beats per minute. I then gave her a magazine and told her to read in time to the metronome, slowly, one syllable per beat. She read for five minutes straight, and stuttered only once. She was amazed.

We experimented, trying various speeds, until we settled on ninety beats per minute as the most satisfactory for ordinary speech. I told her to buy a metronome and practice fifteen minutes a day speaking to its rhythm. She recorded her performance and brought me the tape at her next session. It was not successful. Mrs. J. had been so intent on fighting her speech defect that she was teaching herself to read with a stutter despite the metronome. I taught her the quick relaxation routine—deep breaths held for five or ten seconds and released.

At the next session she was much improved, but she still hesitated before certain words or phrases that had given her trouble in the past. At this point we devoted a session to assertive training in order to build up her self-confidence.

Next we tried to transfer the rhythm of the metronome to the tapping of her fingers or feet. This method sometimes works, but in this case the results were disappointing. She was now speaking fairly smoothly with the metronome, however, so she was ready for the next step.

In the early sixties Dr. Victor Meyer, the English therapist, developed a miniaturized metronome that could be worn like a hearing aid. It could be turned on and off at will, and the tempo was adjustable. American therapist Dr. John Paul Brady of the University of Pennsylvania Medical College has done considerable work with the minimetronome in treating stutterers, so the instrument was available here. Mrs. J. did not object to wearing one, since her hair was long enough to hide it; in fact, she was delighted to have this mobile aid that enabled her to speak with almost no impediment.

Once she had become accustomed to wearing the device, I suggested she turn it off in situations evoking no tension—when she was alone with her husband and little girl, for instance. She was reluctant, because she was still afraid she would stutter in front of her daughter. We then spent several sessions using systematic desensitization to remove the anxiety from having to speak without the metronome. It worked almost 100 percent. She was able to call on her sister and go shopping with the instrument turned off.

When I discharged her, she could meet most situations without her minimetronome and without stuttering, although she still turns on her rhythm-maker at cocktail parties or when she is talking to strangers. Mrs. J. is not only finding life more enjoyable, but she has achieved the goal that brought her to see me in the first place. Her little girl speaks without a stutter.

In Mrs. J.'s therapy, the use of the metronome was complemented by three tried and true techniques of behavior therapy: relaxation, assertive training, and systematic desensitization.

One patient the behavior therapist sees quite often is the fat man or woman who wants to reduce but hasn't the will power to follow a diet. Albert F., whose doctor sent him to see me, was a typical case of obesity.

Albert was twenty-eight years old, stood five feet nine barefooted, and weighed 263 pounds. A high school graduate, he worked as a sporting-goods salesman in a large department store. He played the role expected of the jovial fat man—always laughing, backslapping, and joking with his friends. Actually he was chronically dejected, lonely, and depressed about his appearance. He had trouble finding clothes that fit him and was consequently a rather sloppy dresser. He worried about girls being turned off by his appearance, but not enough, it seemed, to do anything about it. He lived at home with his parents and his sister, who persuaded him to see the family physician, who then referred him to me.

At our first interview I asked Albert if he had ever tried the weight-watching routine. He said he had, several times—once for three days and once for a whole week. He had even starved himself once and lost twenty pounds—which he immediately regained.

Since eating is often a response to anxiety, I asked Albert whether he was particularly tense about something in his life. (If this were the reason for Albert's gluttony, treatment would be aimed at reducing the anxiety that triggered his overeating in the first place.) Was he afraid of some social or sexual situation which drove him to take refuge in obesity? I asked him when he ate and what. What did he feel or think about just before he started gorging? Could he remember any event or situation that could have caused his problem?

Apparently there was no anxiety problem in Albert's case. He had simply acquired an unfortunate habit which was now out of control. Our task was to try to break the behavior pattern.

Albert's pattern was not overeating at meals, but always eating. It was an automatic process with him. He would go to the icebox before sitting down to read the newspaper—or while he was reading, or afterward—and grab a chicken leg or a piece of fruit without realizing what he was doing until he had the snack in his mouth. He kept candy in his room. Cookies or crackers were always on hand. He took potato chips to work and hid them under the counters, where they were constantly available.

Before we worked out a therapeutic routine, I gave him one final test to be sure we were on the right psychological track. I asked him to close his eyes and picture himself as the lean and athletic-looking man he would like to be.

(This test sometimes produces strange results. Once when I asked a portly woman patient to make this visualization, she imagined herself sleek and sexy-looking, but was immediately very upset because all sorts of strange men entered the picture to make passes at her. This was of course a clue to her trouble.) Albert, who was surrounded all day by sports equipment, secretly longed to indulge in some form of athletics. He had no difficulty picturing himself as a slim, hard-bellied boxer fighting for the lightweight championship.

Albert's assignment for the first week was to continue eating whatever and whenever he wanted; but he was to record the time of day, what he ate and how much, and the estimated number of calories consumed, calculated from a table I gave him. At the end of the week he was to bring me his log with the totals. His caloric intake for the week was gargantuan.

The second week's assignment was the same as the first, except that he was to record the time, nature, amount, and caloric content of each item of food *before* eating it, but after it was actually in his hand. This was a first step toward breaking the automatic nature of his habit. Interposing another activity between the impulse to eat and actually eating made him pause and think about what he was doing when he automatically opened the icebox. We were quite successful; his log that week showed four items crossed out; he had decided he didn't want to eat them after all. His caloric intake for the week showed a slight decrease, and he actually lost half a pound. I instructed him to weigh himself daily and bring his figures to my office, where I transferred them to a chart. When the graph finally began to dip a little I gave him positive reinforcement by enthusiastically congratulating him and praising his will power.

The following week we took a step toward self-control.

In addition to keeping records, at some point during each meal he was to put down his fork, take out his watch, and stop eating for exactly two minutes.

To curb his between-meals appetite, I tried aversive therapy. I bought a hand shocker for him, and told him that whenever he caught himself going to the icebox or reaching for potato chips, he was to reach into his pocket and give himself an electric shock. This did not work, however, because in order to avoid the pain of the jolt, he ignored the apparatus. I then switched to aversive imagery —Cautela's covert sensitization. After opening the icebox and before reaching for his between-meals snack, he was to spend ten or fifteen seconds imagining all the unpleasant things about being fat: his sloppy appearance, the girls turning away disgusted, men laughing at him, his shortness of breath climbing subway stairs, the possibility of his having a heart attack in the street, being carted away in an ambulance, dying in a hospital before his family could get to him. Afterward he could stuff himself to his belly's content if he felt like it. That week he showed a significant drop in his caloric intake and the first significant weight loss.

The time had now come for a more strenuous application of the operant methods. After the depressing visualization of the negative approach, Albert needed a little positive reinforcement at home. Since the family's attitude is very important to the patient, I sent written instructions to his parents and sister on how to encourage Albert's progress. When Albert refused a second helping, he was to be cheered and applauded. Every time the weight chart on the wall of the family bathroom took another dip, he was to be greeted with smiles and congratulations.

The aversive visualizations were continued as before, but a covert reinforcement procedure was also introduced. Whenever he resisted an impulse to eat, he was to picture himself as a lean athlete surrounded by beautiful, admiring girls, a picture he found most pleasant. In this way his non-eating was reinforced.

Six or seven weeks into the treatment, his caloric intake had come way down, and he had begun to lose between four and seven pounds a week. Then a crisis arose. I had to be out of town for a few days and we missed one session. When I saw him two weeks later, he was very upset. He had managed to get through the first week all right, but in the middle of the second week he had lapsed into his old habits. He had gained back a few pounds and was thoroughly discouraged.

I reassured him. I told him I was surprised that it had not happened before. After all, he had been trying to break a lifetime habit in a few months, and he could be forgiven for one slip. Let's get a fresh start, I said. We reset our goals.

Originally he had fixed his target at 190 pounds, 73 pounds less than he weighed when we started therapy. I now suggested we aim at a loss of 40 pounds as our first plateau. We reached that mark—223 pounds—in sixteen sessions. I then cut down the frequency of our meetings to every two weeks, later to once a month.

Albert seemed to have arrived at a stalemate when he hit 210 pounds. He was happy, however; he felt better, and he was thrilled at being able to wear a suit that didn't resemble a circus tent. He explored outdoor living. He tried tennis but found he wasn't good at it. He took up deep-sea fishing and enjoyed it. I was then seeing him for a checkup only every three months.

Eventually he attained his goal of 190 pounds. I discharged him, but he repeated our routine whenever he felt he might be slipping. When I called to check with him a year and a half later, he reported he was following his family physician's diet, and weighed a static 185 pounds.

Quite a number of young people come for help because they cannot seem to relate to the world they live in. Some welcome the security of the family, but are unhappy because they are lonely and out of touch with their generation. They lack the simple social skills to belong. I am thinking of people like Tony V.

Tony came to see me because he was afraid he was a homosexual and he didn't want to be. He was about eighteen, a college freshman, of average height and rather thin. He was not a very good student, and had not been accepted at the big city university of his choice. He had to settle for a smaller two-year community college in his native New York. His father, who was a bookkeeper, wanted him to be a certified public accountant, and Tony was willing.

His parents, second-generation Italian-Americans, had moved several times when he was a boy. Tony was too shy to make friends every time he went to a new school; although he wanted desperately to belong, he always seemed to be the outsider. Girls frightened him. Just looking at a girl made him up tight, and he didn't dream of talking to one. Even in his fantasies girls were so anxiety-provoking that when he began masturbating he pictured men instead of girls as his erotic objects.

He convinced himself that he must be homosexual, and was overcome with guilt feelings, which he confided to his mother. She was very much upset and told his father, who was even more upset. His father took him to see the family doctor, who in turn sent him to see me.

Tony said he had had no actual homosexual experiences. He had often bought physical culture magazines with illustrations of nearly naked barrel-chested men with flat bellies and bulging biceps. He would use one of the pictures to excite him while masturbating. He pictured himself in close physical contact with the model, kissing him, wrestling with him, hugging him, but curiously, there was nothing overtly sexual in his fantasies. He seemed to have no interest in the man's genitalia.

One of Tony's classmates excited him very much. The other boy was not aware of Tony's feelings for him, and did not realize he was arousing Tony's jealousy when he spoke of having a date with a girl. Whenever this happened Tony became greatly depressed, and would go home and masturbate. The image of his classmate would occupy his fantasies, but again, although he pictured close physical contact, the genitals did not figure in his imagery.

Tony's pattern did not seem to be that of a true homosexual (if there is such a thing as a true homosexual). I had had a patient with a similar problem before—the painfully shy youth who is so up tight about girls that he substitutes men in his fantasies. It is quite conceivable that an adolescent with this problem may find himself in an overt homosexual situation while he is growing up, but it has been my experience that if he seeks help early enough, the behavior pattern can be modified. Basically his problem—and Tony's—is one of lack of assertion.

As we have seen in previous chapters, a person's behavior can be shaped by modeling on the part of someone else. In Tony's case it was his nonassertive family. His home life was the epitome of monotony and boredom. Weekends were usually taken up with family visits. Occasionally his father would take him to a ball game or they would go bowling, but mostly the time was consumed watching television, doing chores around the house, masturbating, or reading newspapers. He never opened a book. Going to dances was out. Girls were not for him, in any case, since he was a homosexual.

Our first task was to set up an elementary program of assertive training. Tony had to learn such basics as saying "Hi" to the classmate, male or female, in the next seat. We rehearsed possible conversation with strangers. I tried to show him how to go about finding a subject of mutual interest, such as baseball or hockey. As soon as possible I would have to find some group he could join in which he could gain some social experience. Such a group could serve as a laboratory for learning social skills. Tony had heard about a group at his church which held social evenings twice a week. Young people met in the game rooms, played cards, ping-pong, or pool, listened to the jukebox, or just stood around and talked. I told Tony to go down one evening the next week, look around, stay five minutes, and come home.

He did not go. There was no particular reason, he said; he just didn't feel like it. Tony's reaction was familiar; psychologists call it avoidance response. He was afraid some girl would speak to him, and he didn't know what to do if she should. I told him he needn't talk to anyone, but that if someone from his school should recognize and greet him, all he needed to say was "Hi!" Limiting the assignment this way removed some of the anxiety and reduced the need for avoidance.

This time he followed instructions. When he reported to me, I desensitized him to the anxiety of being addressed by strangers of either sex. We also rehearsed scenes of what might happen there, and what he might say while watching ping-pong or listening to music. I told him to stay half an hour.

The next assignment was the same, but this time he stayed an hour and a half. A classmate from his school had invited him to play ping-pong, and he had given a good account of himself.

The following week he joined the club, and began to talk to some of the members when he saw them at school. I explained to him that if he showed a little bit of himself in conversation, he would find that the other fellow would reciprocate. I got him to advance beyond words of one or two syllables. He began to comment on the ping-pong players, comparing their skills. When a girl came up to him after he had finished playing, and said, "That was a good game you just played," instead of merely saying "Thank you" or "Think so?" he learned to say, "He gave me a pretty rough time with that trick serve of his."

After two months of therapy a big breakthrough came. On his own he went to one of the club's Saturday-night parties. A friend of his offered to pick him up at eight o'clock. Tony was sorry he had been so impetuous about accepting, but was determined to go through with it. I tried to desensitize him to some of the situations he was likely to meet, but he went to the party with great trepidation.

He did not dance; he had never learned. He spent most of the evening standing around the buffet table, but he was included in group conversations and met new people. He left the party feeling fine. He talked about it enthusiastically. For four days he had no homosexual fantasies. He masturbated only once during that period, and that time his fantasy was not another male but a girl he had met at the party.

At the end of a year he had grown away from the church club. He joined another informal group made up of young people of both sexes from his school. His homosexual fantasies had disappeared completely. His depression was gone. He got a part-time clerical job, and was about to get his degree in accounting. And he had begun dating girls.

The method most responsible for success in treating Tony is called *in vivo* desensitization. Instead of conquering anxiety by repeated exposure to imaginary tense situations until they have lost their capacity to provoke fear, the patient is led step by step into the fear-provoking circumstances in real life. If he is afraid of meeting strangers, he is deliberately sent into the strange milieu, after preliminary preparation, for short periods that gradually lengthen with each repetition.

Not all lonely young people are that way because of sexual problems or lack of social skills like Tony. Chester L., for example, had been living in a hippie community in New York's East Village for a year when he came to see me. He himself was not a hippie; he could have lived in a moderately plush apartment of his own, but he resented being supported by his father and accepted as little family money as he could to get along. When he came for help, he was so deeply immersed in his sense of failure that he could not even get up the courage or energy to go out and look for a job.

Chester, a tall, slim young man with a delicate physique, had grown up on the West Coast, where his wealthy father ran a highly successful construction firm. A husky, rough-and-tumble character who had started out as a bulldozer pilot and clawed his way to the top of the heap, Mr. L. expected his only son to be the same sort of hairy-chested fighter. Chester did not seem fitted for an athletic career, but his father insisted. He did his best. In high school he went out for football, but was not good at it. After a few weeks, he quit, much to his father's disgust. "You're nothing but a pansy," said Papa, who scoffed when Chester brought home scholarship awards instead of varsity letters.

Chester's mother was no help. She was a borderline psychotic who had been in and out of hospitals most of his life. The boy did his best to please his father. He decided to major in engineering, hoping that he would thus be useful to his father's firm. Chester graduated at the top of his class but did not become an engineer. He was repelled by the idea of cutting his way through the underbrush, climbing mountains, and fording streams with a rugged outdoor gang preparing to build something. Instead he equivocated by coming East to enter a New York college for a graduate degree in engineering. Although his father was not pleased by Chester's decision, he sent his son all the money he needed. Chester took only enough for a spartan existence.

Graduate school was more difficult than college, and the competition frightened him. He couldn't concentrate, and dropped out after the first semester. A series of successive unimportant jobs followed—as a filing clerk, a trainee on Wall Street. None of them lasted more than five weeks, and all of them were tension-provoking. A year passed during which he did nothing but sit in his room daydreaming about nothing, succumbing more and more to his sense of failure. He had no social contacts except a group of hippies who frequented a cheap neighborhood beanery where he ate occasionally. When one of their number left town, they invited Chester to move in with them.

He moved in, but never felt as if he were part of the group. He tried smoking pot, but it did nothing for him. Speed gave him a temporary lift, but left him shattered when it wore off. The hippies accepted him at his own evaluation, left him alone when he wanted to be alone— which was most of the time—and let him join the group conversation when he felt like it. He contributed to the community fund from his allowance.

When I first saw Chester it was obvious that he faced a tremendous problem in assertion. His fear of failure was so great that eight months had passed since he last even looked for a job. He had lost all active contact with reality. We agreed that it was of utmost importance that he find a job. Some element of success was essential to get our therapy moving.

By the third session it was apparent that Chester was not strong enough to withstand the stress and anxiety of job hunting, so we tried a technique my colleague Dr. M. S. Denholtz had used with some success. I had Chester get two copies of the Sunday *New York Times* want-ad section. He was to read it through, stopping to mark each item that held even the least interest for him. Then he was to clip the marked items and mount them on index cards. He had 51 entries when he finished.

He was then to divide the items into three equal piles: those which on second reading held no interest, those which interested him mildly, and those which interested him the most. Creating the three equal piles would force him to make decisions. He was then to discard the least interesting pile, shuffle the index cards, and again make three equal piles and discard the least interesting. He was to repeat the elimination process once more, then to bring me what was left. (I have had some unexpected results with the Denholtz technique. Some patients have found the process of reading, clipping, choosing, and discarding too much trouble. It was less bother, they said, to go out alone and look for a job—and they have done so.)

Chester brought me about a dozen ads offering employment. When we went through the cards together, I was surprised to find that the jobs that attracted him most involved children and teaching. He admitted that his interests had always tended in this direction, but he had ignored them because he feared his father's disapproval. He was now ready to start job hunting.

I sent him to several agencies, warning him that he could expect numerous obstacles, because he had never taken education courses and his engineering degree would have limited appeal to employers seeking teachers. He survived the rejections he received; following a lead he had picked up on his own, he got a volunteer job at a neighborhood settlement house, working three afternoons a week with ten- and eleven-year-olds. He was delighted but apprehensive. But at least he would have specific problems to discuss with me.

Next I advised him to go to several universities to request (in person) catalogues for graduate courses in education. He selected several courses, but found he was not eligible to enroll without having previously completed several undergraduate courses. He registered immediately for the preparatory classes. He was also planning to attend summer sessions, but when he received an offer from the settlement house to act as counselor at its summer boys' camp, he took the job. Although it paid very little, it was recognition, and it was something he liked doing.

Still haunted by the fear of failure, he spent the time remaining before summer camp began with a minigroup I was working with in assertive training. He was eager to become more active conversationally, and to overcome his lack of self-confidence for the summer.

Despite moments of tension, the camp experience was much better than he had anticipated. His employers offered him a part-time job at the settlement house. Again the salary was very low, but the recognition was extremely important to Chester. Moreover, the social contacts involved amounted to a breakthrough.

Until the end of the summer, Chester lived in the East Village with the hippie group. When one of the social workers at the settlement house needed a roommate and invited Chester to move in with him, Chester accepted. Since the colleague did not know that his new roommate had been withdrawn almost to the point of autism, he included him in his normal social activities. People dropped in for an evening of conversation; he went along to return the visit, and even went on double dates his roommate arranged.

Chester still has developed no close relationships with

girls. He is still the quiet one. But he is more confident in his work, which he enjoys. He is continuing his studies in the field of education. While he will never become a complete extrovert, he has come a long way toward a happier life.

The hypochondriac is another frequent candidate for behavior therapy. I treated one imaginary invalid who was an unusual case: he was a physician and should have known better. Dr. H. was thirty-two years old, and had both his military service and his residency behind him. He was married and had two small children, to whom he was very devoted. A physical-medicine and rehabilitation specialist, he was on the staff of a small medical college, in both the clinic and the ward. In addition, he had a small private practice to augment his income and meet the needs of his growing family.

Dr. H.'s extensive medical knowledge was his undoing. He could—and did—make mountains out of medical molehills. He could convince himself that a pain in his shoulder was a prodromal sign of rheumatoid arthritis. An aching big toe was certainly gout or the beginning of a peripheral vascular malady. Pain in his right side was surely carcinoma of the liver. A headache could only be a brain tumor. Rationally he knew he was neurotic, but he couldn't help it. Afraid his fears might be confirmed, he was terrified of going to a colleague with his symptoms.

He came to see me because in order to take out more life insurance, he had to undergo another physical examination, a prospect that panicked him. He had tried for several years to get rid of his fear of doctors through psychoanalysis—without success. He thought behavior therapy might help.

During our first interview I discovered that hypochondria was not Dr. H.'s only problem. He found it exceedingly difficult to leave his family—even for a few hours —to attend a professional meeting. He realized that he needed the contacts and information available at these medical-association sessions, but he still preferred an evening at home.

His devotion to his wife and children seemed exaggerated, especially in view of the fact that while he claimed he was able to communicate freely with his wife, he had never told her about his hypochondria.

First I decided to attack the doctor's fear of doctors through systematic desensitization. After relaxing him, I took him through an imaginary visit to the insurance doctor, who would tell him (in imagination) that he had a progressively disabling heart disease, that he would have to be hospitalized for at least three weeks, that he would be lucky if he did not die of congestive heart failure within three months. After several sessions he was able to envisage the prospect of his own suffering and death with something approaching equanimity. At any rate, he could muster sufficient courage to face the insurance examiner.

The examination showed nothing physically wrong with Dr. H. He was given a clean bill of health and got his insurance, but he was not completely reassured. In fact, after three weeks his fears of illness and visiting a physician returned in full force.

Abandoning systematic desensitization, we moved into the assertive-training approach. If Dr. H. could improve his interpersonal relations by expressing his feelings directly and honestly, he might bring about a more permanent change.

He could never get directly to the point of the matter. He could not, for instance, say in so many words that he would like to see a new film. He would go into a long dissertation on what the film was about, who had recommended it, and why it might be a good idea to go to see it. It took him at least five minutes to tell a story until I showed him how it could be told in thirty seconds.

He responded quickly to assertive treatment; in three or four weeks he was communicating more directly with his wife and colleagues. He was also less afraid to allow his emotions to show. And although the treatment was not specifically directed at his hypochondria, it, too, was definitely on the wane.

At one of our weekly sessions he announced: "I've been thinking about all this, and I've decided to join a Gestalt therapy group." He was not asking for advice; he was stating a fact.

Assertive training had made Dr. H. more aware of his own feelings and less frightened of them. He had heard that Gestalt therapy emphasizes the free expression of feelings and he wanted to become more engaged at that level. There was always the danger that the experience might be too extreme for him at this time, causing him to pull back into his shell. But when he found a Gestalt therapist on his own initiative, I could only wish him luck and let him know he could resume treatment with me should the hypochondria return.

I never saw him again.

Behavior therapy has often been used as an ancillary treatment for medical problems. Patients who need chemotherapy but are afraid to take pills, who are frightened by the thought of a proctoscopic examination, or who are suffering from gallstones but are terrified of the surgeon's scalpel, can usually be helped by reconditioning techniques.

I remember one case of a man who had undergone open-heart surgery. On his tenth postoperative day he was worrying his doctor, his surgeon, and the hospital staff because he was not cooperating in keeping his respiratory passages free of obstruction. The medical team wanted him to cough to keep his lungs and bronchial tubes clear, but he was afraid that the effort of coughing would open up the incisions.

Prior to surgery the patient had been undergoing traditional psychotherapy, but the therapist was unable to help him overcome this postoperative fear. The physician asked me to help. We worked out a hierarchy, a series of imagined scenes ranging from a tiny cough to a long spell of violent coughing, designed to take the anxiety out of the phobic situation. Before the systematic desensitization series I relaxed the patient. I put both routines on tape, and the patient was to listen to them four or five times a day. We never got rid of the fear completely, but at the end of six days our patient could manage a timid, tentative cough which was enough to clear his bronchial tubes and remove him from danger.

While the hypochondriac and the psychosomatic patient are both neurotic to a degree, the psychosomatic's symptoms do require medical attention, even though their cause may be treated by psychotherapy. The most frequent psychosomatic cases I see suffer from either gastric or duodenal ulcers.

Ulcers are popularly regarded as an occupational disease of Madison Avenue. One of my patients was in fact an account executive with a large advertising agency. Morgan F. was a backslapping go-getter—the very incarnation of nervous energy—a sharp dresser who looked younger than his forty-two years. His father, mother, and two brothers were all tense extroverts. Morgan had begun his nonstop rapid-fire conquest of the world in high school. In college he had been a Big Man on Campus—president of his fraternity, editor of the campus paper, among other things.

He had come to New York as a public-relations man and went into advertising several years later. A handsome man, he had a wife, two children, and any number of mistresses.

About ten years earlier Morgan had had a gastric ulcer which had responded to medical treatment. He was getting medical treatment for this one too, but it cramped his Madison Avenue style. Maalox was hardly a proper substitute for a three-martini lunch when he was wooing a prospective client. His doctor had told him that if he did not stick to his diet he might have to face surgery.

We began the relaxation exercises as soon as possible; his muscles were as taut as piano wires. He couldn't sit still. The pressures of his job, he told me, kept his nerves tense all day. He had tried tranquilizers but didn't seem to get any relief.

We estimated his SUD level at 85 when he came in. By the end of the session, which was devoted entirely to relaxation exercises, it had gone down to 40. He was still much too tense. We concentrated on trying to take the tension out of his abdominal muscles—with some success. I recorded the relaxation exercises and gave him the tape cassette to take home. Since Morgan complained of having trouble getting to sleep, I suggested that he play the tape twice after going to bed.

The next week I put him into a light hypnotic trance with a posthypnotic suggestion that he would achieve greater relaxation at home. We could not be sure whether hypnosis had anything to do with it or not, but he reported that he had been able to reduce his SUD level to 5, and that he was sleeping much better.

In subsequent weeks I taught him the quick relaxation routine. Every hour on the hour he was to breathe deeply through the mouth, hold his breath for five or ten seconds, and exhale slowly, letting his body go limp. He was to repeat the process at odd moments if he felt tense.

191

We also tried nonsystematic desensitization. Morgan was to imagine the most upsetting thing that had occurred during the week. He was to picture the worst possible conclusion—even if matters had not actually reached such a catastrophic stage—losing an account with ten million dollars' annual billing and being fired because he had mishandled the situation. He would signal at the first sign of disturbance, and I would then relax him. We did this as many as twenty-five times a session.

Morgan became generally more relaxed, but there was still much work to be done to keep his tensions from returning. Part of his tense, extroverted manner may have been inherited, but he did have an assertive problem. Despite his outgoing and apparently open manner, he had never learned to express himself honestly. As long as this condition continued, I expected him to have trouble with recurring bouts of anxiety. I explained this to him and proposed a program to teach him assertive skills. While he agreed that this was a worthy goal, he was feeling much better—his ulcer was no longer acting up—and he thought he would discontinue treatment for the time being.

Six months later he was back. He was again having trouble sleeping. He was playing the relaxation tapes, but they had lost their magic. He wanted to be relaxed in person, perhaps with a touch of hypnosis. I again broached the subject of assertive training, and he agreed to try it. He didn't follow through, however. Instead he telephoned to say he felt so much better he was not coming.

A year later it was the same story. There was no recurrence of the ulcer, however. Had behavior therapy cured him? Or had the doctor's bland diet and Maalox done the trick?

Whether Morgan was "cured" is an interesting question. Apparently the relaxation exercises were of some help with the ulcer symptoms. The tension and accompanying ulcer symptoms may continue to return, only to disappear again with the application of anxiety-reduction techniques. However, the main behavioral problem—his lack of real assertion—may never be effectively treated. All that has actually been achieved has been to bring a set of symptoms under control. Yet even that much has made the patient's life more comfortable.

Young women who have attained the ripe old age of twenty-five without getting married are also frequently patients. Marilyn M., for example, was a nice-looking Midwesterner who had lived in New York for three years, and enjoyed the excitement of life in the big city. She liked her work as a fabric designer but did not plan to make a career of it. The job was a pleasant stopgap until she was married.

What was wrong with her, Marilyn asked, that she was still single? She had always been popular in high school and college. Her social life was no less lively in New York. She got along well with her colleagues at work and with her friends, but nobody ever got serious with her except men she didn't like.

About four weeks before she came to see me, she had broken up with a man she had been seeing for seven months. He had wanted to marry her, but the more she got to know him the more things she found to dislike about him. He had not seemed too unhappy about the rupture.

From our first interviews, I gathered that much of Marilyn's trouble stemmed from an older sister. The sister was a most unusual person—beautiful, she had married the most eligible bachelor of her home town. She had always been her parents' favorite, and Marilyn had suffered from constant and unfavorable comparison.

Constantly striving to emulate her sister, Marilyn built up what she considered a false front. She found that she could easily "fool" people who didn't know her very well, making them believe that she was just as charming and talented as her older sister. As far as Marilyn was concerned, her vivaciousness, her friendliness, her quick wit and gregariousness were phony. She was pretending to be somebody else.

Two areas of fear were causing her difficulties. Her fear of criticism was based on unfavorable comparison with her sister. She also feared rejection. She had convinced herself that people would eventually see through her pretense, and would say, "Now that I know what you're really like, I want nothing more to do with you."

Since she had worked hard to create this façade, she was determined to protect it. Because she believed she had something to hide, she dared not allow herself to be open and honest with others. The result was a complete breakdown of communications and mounting resentment, anger and irritation.

Therapy was needed on two levels: systematic desensitization to deal with her phobias, and assertive training to build up confidence in her real self as opposed to her façade. I had her list fifteen persons—colleagues at the office, men she went out with, women she knew socially, and finally her parents and older sister—whom we then ranked in the ascending order in which they would provoke anxiety by criticizing her. She was to imagine that each in turn was telling her that he didn't like what she was doing and saying. Her mother and father, of course, came into the picture to tell her how unfavorably she compared with her sister. All this took fourteen sessions.

We spent the next eleven weeks on another list of fifteen, arranged in the ascending order of the disturbing effect of their rejection of Marilyn. She was to listen in imagination until she was not unduly upset by their saying, "No, I can't see you this weekend," or "I really don't like anything about you."

During the same period we spent some time examining her façade to find out how much of it was really phony. We agreed that part of her problem arose from her lack of assertiveness—her inability to speak freely about what she didn't like in a man. For instance, her escort to a Saturday-night party arrived late to pick her up. He had spent the day in the country and was unshaven and sloppily dressed. He offered to go home to clean up, but since it was already late, he said, perhaps she wouldn't mind if they went straight to the party. She did mind, but to avoid offending him, she said, "Come on, let's go as you are. We'll blow their minds." She was extremely uncomfortable all evening, but she put up her usual front.

We considered alternatives to the way she had handled this situation. Suppose she had said, "Look, it won't take long. Why don't we stop at your place on the way, and I'll wait while you shave and change?" What would the escort's response have been? We rehearsed the reactions that would have been most upsetting to Marilyn. Her SUD level rose abruptly as she imagined her escort saying, "I didn't think you would be like that." I had to desensitize her to the tension caused by a rejection of her attempt to be frank.

From the outset I had been encouraging assertion on her part: I tried to get her to express her feelings openly, directly, honestly, and appropriately. I told Marilyn: "You're not getting anywhere anyhow. Marriage is still beyond the horizon. Why don't you experiment? Why not try being honest with your men friends?"

Marilyn opened up with surprising suddenness, as though the idea had not occurred to her before. She began by being honest with herself. She didn't really want to be a fabric designer. She had once worked as a commercial artist and had enjoyed it, so she quit her job and joined an advertising agency as an artist. She was happier generally.

She gained a whole new perspective on herself. She found she didn't have to go through life acting a part, hiding her "real self." The charm she called her façade was actually quite real.

After forty sessions we were both satisfied that she was able to stand on her own feet, and therapy was discontinued. She came back a month or so later. She wasn't getting along with a new boy friend. What was she doing wrong? We analyzed the situation together and concluded that the man, not Marilyn, was at fault. She dropped him.

She has since met a man with whom she could be articulate about her feelings, and who responded in kind. They are now married, and she is seriously considering resuming her original plans for a career: raising a family.

Even more common than the girl seeking marriage is the married couple wondering why their marriage seems headed for the rocks. One such couple, Mr. and Mrs. J., came to me for help.

Mrs. J., a good-looking woman of thirty, had a master's degree in nursing and was working part-time as a psychiatric nurse at a local hospital. She was quiet and introverted and not very articulate about expressing her feelings.

Mr. J. was a thirty-eight-year-old architect. Unlike his wife, he liked big, noisy social events. He could talk endlessly and intelligently about everything in the world—except his personal affairs. He was given to temper outbursts, but they ended quickly. He was not vindictive. He and several friends had formed a new architectural firm that was growing, but was still in a precarious position financially.

Mr. J. claimed that sex was the basis for the impending

failure of their marriage. He was frustrated, he said, by his wife's lack of physical interest. At one point he had actually left her to move in with another woman, who gave him intense sexual satisfaction. He had been happy with this extramarital arrangement, but for his wife's sake had decided to give the marriage another try.

At that point, Mrs. J. wasn't sure she wanted him back. She was hurt and resentful. However, she agreed that they should seek professional help together, so they came to see me.

I determined that phobias were not the foundation of their problem. Mrs. J. was critical of her husband's sexual approach, however, which she said lacked warmth and tenderness. Still, she had never withdrawn physically from his desires. Instead of telling him that she was not in the mood, which was sometimes the case, she passively submitted. Her husband, aware that she was not participating, would upbraid her angrily.

An outburst of this kind occurred after Mr. J. had not come home for dinner two nights running. When he did appear the second midnight, he went right to bed and without preliminaries began making love. When she did not respond, he was furious.

The husband's explanation—which his wife heard for the first time in my office—was this: His firm was engaged in an important building project which involved its financial future. The client was unhappy with the first plans submitted. He and his fellow architects had been working overtime in an effort to produce satisfactory blueprints. When he got home late, he was depressed, afraid the revised plans would be rejected. He wasn't really interested in sex for the sake of sex. What he was seeking was warmth and understanding.

"Did you tell your wife this?" I asked him.

"She should have known," he said.

"Why didn't you ask your husband what was wrong?" I asked Mrs. J.

"It never occurred to me."

They began to see that their problem was lack of communication. If they could both gain skill in assertive behavior, not only the sexual but other aspects of marriage would be favorably affected. They responded eagerly to the prospect of being able to do something practical to improve their marriage.

For fourteen weeks we went through assertive-training routines. They spent several sessions in spontaneous discussion of what each liked and disliked most in the sex relationship. They were encouraged by the way their marriage was improving and enjoyed the feeling of working together.

They came back a few times at three-month intervals for checkups. Last time I heard from them they were getting along fine, in bed and out.

It must be obvious at this point that when I spoke of "common problems" at the beginning of this chapter, I did not mean problems as common as the common cold in January. They are as varied as the techniques that the therapist uses to solve them. Yet they all do have a common origin in the psychology of learning. They all stem either from something the patient has somehow learned to do wrong, or from the lack of something the patient has never learned at all.

11

HOW TO KNOW WHAT'S WRONG WITH YOU

SINCE THE FIRST step in any psychotherapy is diagnosis, this chapter might properly have appeared at the beginning of the book. I have deliberately placed it here, however, so that the reader, by first learning the nature of behavior therapy and its methods, may be able to see how they are applied to specific problems. The purpose of diagnosis is, naturally, to furnish a blueprint for action.

The behavior therapist's approach to diagnosis is very different from that of the traditional methods. The psychoanalyst seeks out root causes. He is interested in early childhood influences. He wants to know about oral, anal, or Oedipal approaches, breast feeding, toilet training, and early childhood masturbation. Present symptoms are important to the psychoanalyst only as they shed light on the patient's unconscious, where, he says, the problem originates.

The behavior therapist stands this concept on its head. Childhood development is almost certainly of some importance in considering adult actions, but it is essentially irrelevant to behavior therapy. The behavior therapist is interested in what is disturbing the patient today, whether it is an outward expression of not getting along well with other people, or an internal expression of some fear. First of all he tries to see exactly what the problem is, and second, to determine what specific behavior or behaviors must be changed to resolve it.

The behavior therapist usually has no trouble getting at the facts that are readily available. The claustrophobic who consults a behavior therapist, for instance, makes no secret of his fears or what he does about them. If the patient is sexually impotent, he will tell you what is wrong, and two thirds of the time, as Masters and Johnson have pointed out in their scholarly work on human sexual inadequacy, sexual failure has been caused by fear of sexual failure.

The behavior therapist begins his diagnostic interview by asking his patient what is wrong, and most of the time the patient will tell him outright. He is depressed, or he is having trouble with his wife, or he is afraid of flying. Let me illustrate.

Bob S. was a big, husky, healthy-looking lad of twenty-two, originally from Minneapolis. He had an engineering degree from a Boston university, and now worked as a technical editor for a New York publisher. When Bob came into my study I was struck by his manner. He walked as stiffly as a robot, and I thought he might be suffering from some central nervous system ailment. He had been referred to me by a competent internist, however, who would have spotted any pathological trauma. As he sat down, he was so tense that I thought he was on the verge of tears.

What was his problem? He was terribly depressed. He had always loved his work, but now he hated to go to the office in the morning. In fact, he hated to get up and face another day.

I probed into his background. He had always been shy and had never had many friends. Although he shared an apartment with another man, it was purely a matter of economics and convenience. The acute depression that had hit him three or four weeks ago was something he could not face any longer.

"Have you any idea what set this off?" I asked.

"I certainly do," he replied. About six months ago he had become intimately involved with a girl. He thought he was in love with her, and she seemed to reciprocate his feelings. There was only one drawback: she was living with another man while she was going out with Bob. She wanted to get rid of the other man and marry Bob, she told him. Unknown to Bob, she kept the other man aware of the progress of her affair with Bob in detail.

Bob was living on Cloud Nine. He had never known such a blissful feeling of belonging to someone who loved him and who in turn seemed to belong to him.

Out of the blue the girl telephoned him one night, apparently with the boy friend on another extension. She wanted to say goodbye; she and the boy friend were going to be married. She had never really loved Bob, she said, but had gone through the motions just to make the boy friend jealous enough to marry her.

A few nights later she called again to rub it in. She didn't want Bob to think she had said what she did only because her boy friend was on the other extension. She had meant it. How could Bob think she had really fallen for him?

Under the circumstances, Bob's acute depression was understandable.

The diagnosis was fairly simple. Bob's long-term problem was lack of assertion. He was afraid to let his bottled-up emotions come out. This reluctance stemmed from Bob's fear of anger and aggressiveness. However, his immediate problem was fear of loneliness, and the immediate treatment was intensive relaxation and systematic desensitization. We started therapy during the first session by setting up a hierarchy of anxiety-evoking situations having to do with being alone. There was no need to dig into Bob's childhood fantasies in order to diagnose his problem. I am confident that the plan we formulated at that initial interview will work out well.

How do I know my diagnosis is correct? If the treatment brings successful results, I am right. If it doesn't, we start again from scratch.

It is sometimes more difficult to get to the core of the problem than was the case with Bob. Take the case of Frances F., for instance.

Frances, an attractive girl in her late twenties, was a smart dresser with style and a social life to match. She had a good job with a large New York department store as buyer of women's clothes. Her problem: she wanted to get married; why couldn't she?

The answer to the question was not apparent, and at first I could get no clues from Frances. She had an active social life, many good friends, exciting vacations, a beautiful apartment, and no sexual hangups. She enjoyed sex, but was not promiscuous. She had been going with one man for some five years, even though she knew he had no intention of marrying her. He was too frightened of assuming adult responsibilities to take such an independent step as marriage.

After several sessions I was able to formulate Frances's problem. Her basic fear was twofold. First, she was afraid of rejection by men. This was a rather peculiar kind of fear, which centered around her father, who had rejected the self-sufficient woman Frances had apparently become. This fear had been generalized to the possibility of rejection by all men. She believed that only by giving up the self-sufficiency so important to her could she avoid this rejection. She felt safe with her current beau; even if he would not marry her, at least he did not repudiate her—which led to her second problem. If Frances wanted to get married she would have to break off her present liaison, and she was afraid that if she lost him, she would never find someone who would marry her. I had to desensitize her to freeing herself from her current boy friend so she could date other men.

In Frances's case, again, I was able to treat her on the basis of information that was all in her conscious.

Sometimes the patient is not aware of what really causes his phobia, and the therapist presents the wrong scenes for him to visualize in the process of desensitization. Mrs. S., who was referred to me by her psychoanalyst, was such a case.

"For God's sake," the analyst pleaded, "will you get rid of her fear of sailboats so we can get on with her analysis?"

It seems that Mr. S. was an enthusiastic yachtsman. He insisted that his wife, who hated sailing, accompany him, and she did, but it was such a traumatic experience that she could talk about nothing else during her sessions with her analyst. They were making no progress.

At our first session Mrs. S. told me that her husband delighted in running close to the wind, and she became particularly terrified when he sailed his lee rail under and the deck slanted steeply.

I constructed a hierarchy on the basis of her fear of the boat's heeling over. First I asked her to picture the boat leaning at five degrees, then ten, fifteen, twenty. Her SUD level declined as we repeated visualizations of the boat leaning at five, ten, and fifteen degrees. Beyond that angle, however, she could not be relaxed; sixteen degrees produced tension. Apparently I was on the wrong track.

We tried dealing with the fear vicariously, a technique that sometimes reduces anxiety to a level low enough to proceed with desensitization. I had her visualize boats heeling at twenty degrees, showed her movies of other boats, then her husband's boat, doing this. Twenty-two sessions showed no progress.

Finally I shifted the scenes to the fear of water and the fear of drowning. In three sessions she was completely desensitized.

I have since heard from Mrs. S. that she has come to enjoy sailing. Once she fell asleep while the boat was practically standing on its beam-ends. And she even goes forward to handle the lines during a squall.

Since behavior therapy is a relatively new and little-known system of treatment, I always encourage my patients to read books on the subject. When they know what I am looking for in order to make a diagnosis, they can help a great deal in the formulation of their own treatment plan. Bertie B. was such a case.

Bertie had been in psychoanalysis for two years and was discouraged by his lack of progress. When he called me for an appointment, I immediately phoned his analyst, who counseled against the projected change. Bertie, he said, was on the verge of a breakthrough; to switch therapies now would be a serious mistake. I agreed and explained the situation to Bertie. Bertie, however, was determined to try behavior therapy. Inasmuch as he had the right to choose the sort of treatment he wanted, I then accepted him.

Bertie had a problem with homosexuality. He also had heterosexual leanings, but was never comfortable dating girls. He wanted to give up his homosexual relations, however, before they determined his life pattern. His problem seemed to be threefold: 1) Fear of sex. 2) Fear of being dominated by women. 3) Fear of being rejected by women.

First I tried attacking his fear of women through systematic desensitization. He did not respond. Bertie was one of those individuals who do not experience anxiety reactions to anxiety-provoking scenes. Systematic desensitization would not work with him, so I decided to try an aversion approach, starting with the next session.

At the next session, however, he came in with his own formulation of his problem. "You know, I've been reading about behavior therapy," he said, "and I think I know what my trouble is. It's a problem of assertion. I've just never learned to speak up openly, honestly, and appropriately to anyone, man or woman." He illustrated with a series of specific incidents.

He was right. He had picked up the standard definition of the nonassertive person, and assertive training was definitely indicated. We switched treatment, and by the next session the change in his attitude was already apparent.

Another patient who wanted to mastermind at least part of her therapy was Marilou G., a very pretty girl in her early twenties. "It is obvious that my problem is depression," she said as she walked into my study the first time, "but before I begin therapy with you, I want your assurance that you will confine your treatment to that aspect of my life. I am a lesbian, and I am quite happy with my way of life. Will you accept me on those terms?"

I agreed to treat only her depression if it was not connected with sex. Apparently it was not.

Marilou had dropped out of college after her second year because she had flunked one course and got low marks in the others. For several years she had been working as a salesclerk in a New York department store, and had recently been offered a promotion to assistant buyer. Whenever she thought about accepting or turning down the offer of promotion, she became very depressed. Why?

When I asked, she said she had considered her job as a salesgirl only temporary. She really wanted to go back and finish college. A promotion represented the first step toward a permanent career in merchandising; she might never go back to school. She would be wasting her life.

Then why didn't she go back? She was afraid she couldn't make the grade. With her problem thus defined, I desensitized her to the fear of academic failure. She quit her job and re-entered college. She got through her junior year with a B average. As far as I know she is still happily homosexual.

The behavior therapist is sometimes consulted in cases in which assertive training is really an education in the ABCs of elementary social practices. I am thinking of people like Henry J., a brilliant lawyer in his mid-fifties. When he came to consult me he had been working for a prestigious law firm for thirty years.

Henry was highly regarded by his employers. They would give him a legal problem, he would research the laws concerned, prepare arguments, and draw up intelligent briefs. However, he was completely inept in dealing with other people. His career had been spent in the law library.

Henry was an only child. His father had died when he was a boy and he had been raised by his mother, who proceeded to build her whole life around him. He came home to have lunch with her while he was in school. In high school he had few friends. He finished college and law school with honors—but without once dating a girl. Because of his academic distinction he was instantly hired by the important law firm. He wouldn't have had the nerve to ask for a raise, but he was automatically given a salary boost every year or so until he was earning a handsome paycheck.

Once he was making enough money to support a wife, his mother picked out a suitable woman for him to marry.

The couple made their home with his mother. He never took a vacation without either his wife or mother or both. When both his mother and his wife died within a short time of each other, Henry had to learn to live for himself, and he had not the slightest notion how to start. He came to me for help.

Henry wanted to remarry, but he did not know how to go about it. Having lived in a closed society for half a century, he was completely ignorant of the rules, customs, and usages of the complex world in which he now found himself. He refused all invitations to dinner, for example, because he didn't know how to be the extra man.

Henry's therapy consisted of instruction in the simple amenities. What should he wear to a dinner party? Should he bring the hostess flowers or a bottle of wine? If the hostess opened the door for him, he supposed he should say "Good evening. It was nice of you to invite me," but what should he say if a maid opened the door? Since he never touched alcohol, what should he do if he were offered a cocktail? Should he simply refuse, or would it be correct to say he would rather have ginger ale? If paired with a woman at the dinner table, what should he talk about? Would he be expected to take her home? Should he kiss her goodnight? Would he be expected to go to bed with her?

Well embarked on his adult education, he started accepting invitations, and eventually met a possessive, matronly woman who would run his life for him as his wife and mother had always done. He married her and settled down to the kind of life he had always known.

Some may ask whether Henry was really helped. No attempt was made to change his dependent, withdrawn life. But Henry was happy. If he asked himself, "Am I getting what I want out of life?" he would have to say yes. The man who answers no must ask further questions of himself. "Why not? What am I doing wrong?"

Take the case of the compulsive philanderer. Luke was a married man with several children, but he couldn't stay home nights. His wife was not fooled by his phone calls about having to work late at the office, or his frequent weekend business trips. Although he got little satisfaction from his marital relationship, he got even less satisfaction from playing Lothario.

When his wife's complaints kept him at home occasionally, he insisted on having a houseful of people. Left alone, he was unhappy. He couldn't read. He ignored his children. At his wife's insistence he came to see me to try to find out why he was not getting what he wanted out of life.

His basic problem seemed to be a fear of being alone. I began desensitizing him and he responded quite well. I then discovered he had a problem in assertion.

Luke and a partner ran a moderately successful accounting firm. Luke, however, lacked assertion in dealing with clients. He was unable to dun them for overdue bills. Assertive training was added to our program. I gave him limited tasks to perform. "Tomorrow," I told him, "you must telephone X and say, 'I'm calling about that bill you owe us. It's six months overdue now and I wonder when we might expect payment.'" We rehearsed the scene until he could do it without tension. The following day he was to make the actual call.

Both lines of therapy were successful. He spoke up to his clients and lost the compulsion to assert himself by chasing girls. He no longer feared loneliness, began to enjoy his children, and was able to spend an evening at home without filling the house with friends and strangers.

Like Luke, many people are overwhelmed by their problems because they cannot decide exactly which ones they want to solve. They are surprised to discover that stating the problem in its simplest terms often leads to the solution.

Getting at the specifics of a problem is not always easy. I usually group questions systematically around four central areas. I will first list the areas and then expand on them as I often do with patients.

1) What is your problem? How intense is it? To what extent is it disruptive?

2) When did the trouble start? Was some change going on in your life at the time? What were the exact circumstances under which the trouble first occurred?

3) When is the problem most disturbing? When least?

4) Is there a specific fear or other disturbing emotion connected with your problem? What is the worst outcome you might anticipate?

In examining these questions with a patient, I try to suggest certain guidelines and attitudes. I don't always put them into so many words—many of the guidelines are communicated by implication—but I will try here to spell out my intent in each area.

1) Describe the problem just as it appears to you. Don't try to interpret, especially in terms of unconscious drives, mystical forces, or the forgotten past. Be frank with yourself, and be specific. If you are afraid of your boss, don't say you have a problem with authority or that you may have an unresolved Oedipus complex. Say, "I'm afraid to ask my boss for a raise," or "I make mistakes every time my boss comes into the room."

In answering the questions relating to the extent and intensity of the problem, you must not draw a false general conclusion from a true individual instance. For example, if your problem is fear of sex, it makes an enormous difference in its possible solution whether you are frightened of sex to the extent that a) you do not enjoy sex, b) you are impotent (or frigid) at times, c) you avoid marriage, d) you avoid the opposite sex completely, or e) you are afraid of becoming homosexual.

Whether the problem is disrupting your life or whether you can still live with it is a subjective appraisal that you alone can make accurately.

2) Questions about when your trouble started and what changes took place in your daily habits or your social and economic life at the time are extremely important in providing diagnostic clues. Answers focusing on specific behavior and attending circumstances often yield simple solutions to apparently complex problems. Let me illustrate.

A young college instructor came to see me because he had begun to wonder if he was in the wrong profession. He had always enjoyed teaching, but about a year before I saw him he had become jumpy and depressed. During the whole semester the mere thought of appearing before his classes aroused such anxiety that he perspired, stammered, and gave a generally unsatisfactory performance. He was seriously considering giving up his academic career and taking a job in industry.

When did his problem begin? At about the time he started working on his doctoral thesis. What changes occurred in his life at this time? When he began research for his thesis the pressure started building up and he neglected his classroom routine. He had even stopped preparing his lectures, depending instead on off-the-cuff pontification. And he had fallen far behind in grading his written assignments. His tensions had increased in direct proportion to the dimensions of the pile of uncorrected papers on his desk. The thought of confronting his students unprepared made him even more tense, and finally he found it impossible to organize his lectures.

Once he realized that the change in his routine was at the root of his problem, he was able to revert to his previous pattern of academic behavior. The following semester he went back to his classes with his old enthusiasm.

3) The when-worst-when-least questions represent a different approach to the basic conditions generating anxiety. The answers are particularly illuminating to the therapist and may be equally useful to the patient. The when-worst answer often furnishes a clue to the underlying tensions, while the when-least answer may highlight areas of strength to serve as a starting point in a therapy program.

One patient of mine was so terrified of airplanes that merely hearing one overhead would make her cringe. She was only slightly upset, however, by looking at a picture of a plane in a magazine, and that became the starting point of a desensitization series to overcome her phobia.

Another patient, a thirty-eight-year-old married man who seemed perfectly competent socially, was sexually inadequate. He had difficulty maintaining an erection, and had rarely achieved satisfactory intercourse during the past four years. His trouble had begun at a time when he had taken a new job and it wasn't going very well. This man's answers to the worst-least question were quite revealing. He was most disturbed when his wife was very excited and expected him to provide satisfaction—which, not unexpectedly, was when anxiety drove him to premature ejaculation. He was least troubled early in the morning when he was relaxed after a good night's sleep.

His problem was that he brought a generalized state of tension to the sexual situation. The initial tension was increased by his wife's eagerness—and led to failure. In the morning, when the initial tension was not present, he had no trouble. On the basis of the patient's answers to the worst-least questions, we were able to devise a plan of treatment which included a reduction of job tensions.

4) The first part of this question—name the specific fear connected with your problem—may seem at first glance to

211

be a repetition of the first question, to describe your problem. It is not. It asks for disturbing emotions which may help identify the core fear, particularly if that fear is not the one you indicate in your final answer: the worst that could happen to you. For instance, the partially impotent husband mentioned in No. 3 worried that his wife, frustrated by his impotence, will tell his friends that he is not much of a man. The very worst that could happen, however, was that his wife would leave him.

Your answer to the last part—what is the worst outcome you might anticipate?—may strike you as silly or trivial. Say it anyway. If it seems silly to you when you put it into words—if you are able to say "Is this all I've been afraid of?"—you may be able to laugh off your anxiety and dispose of your problem spontaneously. In any event, you now have a focus for treatment.

Once the problem has been defined and the behavior to be changed has been clarified, a specific program of treatment emerges. Although the treatment procedures may become quite complex, they can usually be fitted into one of the following classifications: relaxation, assertion, breaking old habits, learning new habits, and conquering phobias —each of which we have discussed in previous chapters.

Learning to relax is an adjunct to many other techniques of behavior therapy. It is directly helpful in approaching specific problems such as insomnia, inability to concentrate, and subjective loss of control. If you can acquire the ability to relax, you will find it easier to cope with the tensions of a disturbing situation without feeling completely helpless. Relaxation exercises are described in Chapter 2 and in the appendix.

Assertion. If the heart of your problem is the inability to express your innermost thoughts and feelings openly, honestly, and appropriately—if you are unable to be the real

You when stung by anger or moved by tenderness, you probably need assertive training. Read Chapter 4 again. The variations on the technique of dialogue between a husband and wife on the verge of separation may help you pinpoint other problems in this area. A sympathetic spouse could help you in behavior rehearsal to meet certain confrontations. Examine this chapter very carefully if your troubles include an unsatisfactory social life, marital misunderstanding, resentment at being pushed around, angry outbursts, or periods of depression. Assertive exercises will help you gain new respect—from yourself, as well as from others.

Breaking old habits. Overeating, drinking too much, and many addictions are real problems because people have learned an undesirable habit and can't break it. Compulsive gambling and some abnormal sexual behavior are more extreme examples of the same inappropriate learning process. Aversion techniques may not be of much use without professional supervision for one seeking to break these habits, although both thought-stopping and the hand shocker have been used at home with some success.

Learning new habits. It is not always necessary to erase bad habits in order to correct problem behavior. Sometimes a problem arises because an individual has simply not learned the proper habits to cope with it.

One of my patients was a twenty-year-old college student who could not make himself study. At the beginning of each semester he was full of good resolutions. For two weeks he kept up with his homework, but from that point until about ten days before final examinations he never opened a book. At the last minute he would burn the midnight oil and cram for long hours. There was no anxiety connected with his failure to study—he had simply never learned good study habits—but there *was* anxiety connected with his fear of flunking the exam. Using operant techniques, the therapist can help him learn good study habits.

Conquering phobias. The patient is encouraged to examine for himself and with the therapist the specific fears (or other disturbed feelings) he associates with his problem situation. We have to determine if the fear causes the problem or results from it. Usually the fear causes the problem. The withdrawn person, for instance, is frightened of being rejected. His fear causes him to avoid people. Thus his basic fear is not of people but of being rejected. The practical value of assuming this causal relationship is that desensitization is quite effective in doing away with the original fear. We can find out soon enough whether or not we are right.

To uncover the specific behavior patterns that underlie a problem, the behavior therapist uses his clinical knowledge and interviewing techniques, sometimes supplemented by questionnaires designed for this particular purpose. Once these patterns are clearly seen, the general treatment procedures follow logically. Knowing what is wrong is more than half the battle.

12

A LESS NEUROTIC TOMORROW

SO FAR IN THIS BOOK I have tried to illuminate the definition of behavior therapy as it appears in the first chapter: a series of techniques for changing behavior patterns that are affecting people's lives unfavorably. While this describes the activities of the practicing clinician, it hardly touches the theory or the philosophy of the developing science. Neither does it look ahead to the crossroads being approached by all psychotherapy in the computer age. I should therefore like to add a corollary:

Behavior therapy is a revolutionary way of looking at people and their problems.

The reader who has come this far, particularly if he is becoming acquainted with behavior therapy for the first time, can readily understand the application of the term "revolutionary." For two generations most of us have been conditioned to think of psychotherapy in terms of deep-seated problems, core conflicts, and unconscious impulses. It is hard to extinguish these habits of thought. Personally I still have trouble with my own analytically oriented conditioning, and the perceptive reader can probably pick out spots in this book where I have lapsed into traditional phraseology. The idea of treating neurotics without recourse to traditional concepts is little short of unbelievable. And for me to say, as many of my behavioral colleagues do, that there are no neurotics—only people who have learned unadaptive behavior patterns—would be sheer heresy.

Yet we have just read about many people who were

changed without a single reference to unconscious conflicts or infantile fantasies. Some of their problems were minor; but even beyond the relief of distress, discomfort, or inconvenience, solving a minor problem may bring about a complete change in life-style. I once had as patient a college girl who had the "simple" fear of wetting herself in public. The fear made an emotional mess of her life. She was afraid of her own shadow, afraid to go out, afraid of people. Getting rid of the fear changed her life radically. She discovered a sense of adventure, traveled in Europe, joined an archeological project in Athens, and is learning Greek. Hers is by no means an unusual outcome in the history of behavior therapy's treatment of "minor" problems.

"But," the analytically conditioned reader may protest, "can you bring about real changes without changing the basic personality?"

The question is reasonable until we ask for the meaning of "basic personality" and "real." Contemporary research suggests that there are two aspects of personality.

First there is the temperamental aspect—temperament in the original sense of physical and mental qualities—which includes sensitivity to stimulation, strength and speed of reactions, and general moods. These characteristics are biological and evidence is mounting that they may be inherited. Neither psychoanalysis nor behavior therapy can change these traits, although drug-induced biochemical changes may have some influence.

The second aspect of personality consists of a series of behavior patterns, both external acts and internal emotions and thoughts, all of which have been influenced by life experiences. Here learning plays a role. Some behavioral psychologists maintain that personality is the sum total of these learned habits. If we change these habits through the technology of learning, then personality also is changed.

But is the change "real"? The behavior therapist answers: "Does not feeling differently, acting differently, living a different life pattern than before treatment constitute real change?" No, says our critical reader. If the deep-seated conflicts have not been resolved, the change can only be illusory. The original symptom will come back or a substitute symptom will develop.

The truth or falsity of this empirical question can be determined only through the hard data of empirical research. Sophisticated research into the number of times symptoms actually return is now being done, and the final answer is not yet in. But the evidence to date is overwhelmingly one-sided: when the methods of behavior therapy are used, the return or substitution of symptoms is extremely rare.

Our critical reader is still not satisfied. Can the change be real, he asks, if we don't understand what motivated the behavior in the first place? Can the single girl really free herself to marry if she doesn't understand her incestuous feelings about her father? Can the impotent man really fulfill himself sexually if he has no insight into his castration fears? Can the fat man stick to his diet if he doesn't understand the childhood deprivation that heightened his oral needs? The answer to all these questions is an unequivocal yes! All these changes can be brought about without understanding of and without insight into first causes. Hard facts have proved this indisputably.

At this point the critical reader may justifiably ask: Where *are* these hard facts? In this book, which is more about the art than the science of behavior therapy, I have interspersed a bit of theory among the factual descriptions of many cases. The stories are true, except for the names and other clues to the identity of patients, which have been disguised, but they do not constitute hard, scientific fact. Scientists call these case histories "anecdotal evidence" and consider them valueless as proof of any theory, treatment, or outcome, whether they concern behavior therapy, psychoanalysis, or other fields of scientific inquiry. Case histories illustrate; they do not prove.

However, proof of the efficacy of behavior therapy does not rest on stories or on clinical experience. It does not rest on a therapist's impression or a patient's statement. It *does* rest on a large and expanding body of hard research data.

First, extensive research is being done on learning and the conditions that influence it. For nearly a century, scientists have probed the mechanics of acquiring and eliminating behavior patterns, or habits. The names of Pavlov and Skinner, giants in the field, head a list of more than a thousand scientists who have established the foundation on which the techniques of behavior therapy are based.

Even at this early stage of its development, it is probably fair to say that more careful experimentation has been done in behavior therapy than in all the other areas of psychotherapy combined. As in any experimental area, some of the work is important, some trivial. Some of it is plodding and pedestrian, some highly imaginative and creative. Some is sloppy, but most of it meets the highest standards of experimental psychology. Every technique is eventually put to the test.

The scientific assay of systematic desensitization exemplifies the method. The first challenge the experimenters faced was to determine objectively whether or not the technique worked. Testimony of the patient was not considered evidence. Posttherapy tests were made in a life situation wherever possible. If the subject was too frightened to pick up a harmless snake before desensitization, could he do it afterward? He could. If a student was panicked by anxiety during mid-term examinations, could removing the anxiety by desensitization cause his grades to improve? It could and did. For the very first time, behavior therapists were demonstrating an effective treatment method that would work with predictable results.

Having proved that the method worked, at least in these cases, experimenters went on to determine which factors were responsible. Perhaps the therapist was the key. A different therapist was tried for each desensitization session. Experiments were performed without a therapist; instructions were given via audio tape. These variations made no difference in the results. The fears gave way to desensitization, even independently of a therapist.

Next, experimenters investigated the part played by the patient in composing the hierarchy used. Result: It doesn't seem to matter whether the patient participates in building the hierarchy or uses one devised by the therapist alone. Desensitization does not seem to work, however, if the patient pictures scenes irrelevant to his fears, even while relaxed, or if he pictures relevant scenes while he is *not* relaxed. And relaxation may not be the only effective counteranxiety method. Very mild electric shocks, isometric exercises, pounding a table—perhaps any disruption interposed between stimulus and anxiety reaction—may work, according to some experimenters.

Still other aspects of systematic desensitization are being studied carefully. Certain physiological changes accompany the process of desensitization. Some evidence indicates that desensitization may work better in groups than in individual sessions. While past experiments seemed to indicate that the more a patient expected of desensitization, the less successful the outcome, a more recent study found no relationship between patient expectation and results.

Other techniques of behavior therapy are being subjected to close scrutiny. The operant procedures are being investigated. The conditions under which positive reinforcement is given are described in detail. The behavior of deeply disturbed patients in hospitals is recorded quantitatively. For example, if a patient spends 84 percent of his time sitting on his bed before operant therapy is begun, and only 11 percent after he gets reinforcement, the figures are meaningful. If he has averaged four interactions with other patients on days before therapy, and sixty-three inter-actions afterward, this is objective evidence of successful treatment.

Assertive training is more complex, more unsystematic, and less standardized than other techniques. In spite of the difficulties involved in measuring its success or failure, it, too, is being evaluated under scientific conditions.

One of the most encouraging aspects of behavior ther-apy's critical self-examination, particularly in terms of the future, is the close cooperation between clinician and ex-perimenter. The clinician has an idea, tries it out, reports it. The experimenter tests it, and then confirms, rejects, or modifies the clinical experience. Or vice versa. The experi-menter reports an unusual finding or a change in method, and the clinician tests it to discover whether or not it helps his patients.

Perhaps by this time the critical reader is ready to agree that enough objective evidence exists of behavior therapy's success in bringing about changes in behavior. These changes might occur, he says, not only without the patient's "gaining insight," but even without his being aware of changing. Ethical questions arise: Isn't this brainwashing? Or couldn't it lead to brainwashing? Is it moral to change a habit that the patient does not want changed?

It does happen that psychological principles are used for nontherapeutic purposes. Concepts—even psychoana-lytical concepts—are employed to sell people goods they don't particularly want and political candidates they had not previously admired. For commercial purposes, habits of questionable health value—smoking, for example—are linked to pleasant associations like romance or rustic beauty.

As techniques for changing behavior become more and more effective, it becomes more and more possible to manipulate people, sometimes through behavioral methods.

The strict ethics of the individual clinician will protect his own patients to a large extent. (There has even been debate about the ethics of using aversive methods; some of us were uneasy about aversion until we saw its benefits.) But who will protect the public from uncontrolled manipulation? Some of the interests involved have made first attempts to face the problem, but the ultimate answers must lie with society itself.

Moving to another area of controversy—one we have already touched on briefly—the critical reader may ask: Does the fact that behavior-therapy techniques can change people without resorting to complex psychoanalytical concepts mean that Freud was wrong? Not at all. Behavior therapists have not tested Freud's formulations. In many cases they deal with, psychoanalytic theory is irrelevant, or they can get along without it. Whether Freud was right or wrong would not affect the methods or results of behavior therapy.

Although there are sharp differences on certain points of theory between analysts and behavior therapists, the framework of psychoanalytical thinking is sufficiently broad and flexible to absorb new findings without surrendering any of its fundamentals. Some psychoanalysts are already beginning to incorporate behavior techniques into their work.

As behavior therapists gain experience with a broader variety of people, we may find that the conditioning techniques, while still necessary, are not sufficient. Under some circumstances we may have to deal with the psychological organization of the individual—the interrelations among behavior patterns—in order to bring about desired changes. This organization may be based on the ideas of Freud or it may follow a completely different principle.

A final practical question remains. How can a person tell whether behavior therapy or one of the traditional forms of treatment would benefit him more? Although I have found no hard fact on which to base an answer, the best advice I can give is to try behavior therapy first. If it is going to work, the results will usually be seen in a relatively short time and the changes should be obvious. If it doesn't work—and there are certainly failures in behavior therapy—there will still be time to try some other approach.

For the moment there is no central register of behavior therapists available for those seeking consultation. The rosters of associations offer no certification of competence. I suggest, therefore, that anyone seeking help through behavior therapy contact the psychology department at the college or university nearest him. Any member of the psychology faculty should be able to furnish the name of a therapist.

Fortunately, the growing acceptance of behavior therapy, both within the profession and by the public in general, has led to the establishment of training centers for conditioned-reflex therapy at many universities and medical schools. In the immediate future this will relieve the current shortage of trained behavior therapists and make the techniques more readily available. In the short run we may also look for an increased use of the operant methods, radical changes in assertive-training methods, and some modification of other techniques. In the longer run, the only statement I can make with certainty is that ten years from now we will not recognize behavior therapy, so great will be the changes.

However, today's goals may still apply: a life of self-respect and closeness to others, freedom from irrational fears, the capacity to meet life's creative challenges. Behavior therapy will provide much of the help many of us need.

APPENDIX A
Relaxation Exercises

The following is the text of a tape recording made during a relaxation session and given to patients to take home. Readers who wish to record it for their own use should have it read by a person whose voice can on demand assume a lulling quality. The passages referring to the tensing of the muscles should be read briskly. Those calling for relaxation are read in a slow, soothing, almost musical cadence that carries some element of hypnotism.

Lie down. Your eyes are closed. Your arms are at your sides, your fingers open. Get yourself good and comfortable. If stray thoughts enter your mind, say to yourself, STOP. Push them away and concentrate on what we are doing . . .

The first thing to do is tighten the muscles in the lower part of your body. Turn your feet inward, pigeon-toed, heels slightly apart. Curl your toes tightly, bend your feet downward away from you . . . now upward toward you . . . this tightens the muscles along your shins and in your calves . . . At the same time tighten up your thighs, tighten up the muscles of your buttocks, and the muscles around your anus . . . not so tight that they are strained, but tight enough to feel the tension . . . Study it, study the tension . . . Tense, tense, tense . . . (*Five-second pause*)

Now relax . . . Just feel the tension flow out . . . Concentrate on relaxing the muscles of your toes . . . Relax the muscles of your legs . . . Relax the muscles of your thighs . . . Relax your buttocks, the muscles around your anus . . . Now concentrate on each part of your body as I name it . . . Toes relaxed . . . legs relaxed . . . thighs relaxed . . . muscles of your buttocks . . . relaxed . . . All the tension out . . . (*Ten-second pause*)

Now tighten up the muscles of your abdomen. Make the muscles of your abdomen as taut as if a child were going to shove a football into your stomach . . . Get them good and tight . . . Study the tension . . . Feel where the tension is . . . Hold it for ten seconds . . . Hold it . . . Tense . . . tense . . . tense . . .

And now relax . . . Relax the muscles of your abdomen . . . Let them go . . . Try to relax the muscles deep inside your abdomen . . . the muscles of your gut . . . Let them go . . . You are more and more and more relaxed . . . (*Ten-second pause*)

And now the muscles of your back . . . Arch your back . . . arch the small of your back until you feel the tension build . . . Try to locate the tension . . . There are two long muscle columns alongside your spine . . . You may feel the tension there . . . Wherever it is get to know the feel of tension . . . Your back is tense . . . tense . . . tense . . .

And now relax . . . Relax the muscles of your back . . . Let them go . . . Let all the tension out . . . Your back feels limp and heavy . . . Let it stay that way . . . More and more and more relaxed . . . (*Ten-second pause*)

And now the muscles of your chest . . . Take a deep breath and hold it . . . Just keep on holding it . . . Five seconds . . . Notice as you hold your breath the tension begins to build up . . . Note the tension in your chest muscles . . . Study where it is . . . Ten seconds . . . Keep holding your breath . . . Recognize the feeling of tension . . . Fifteen seconds . . . Now slowly, as slowly as you can, let your breath out . . . Slowly . . . Now breathe

easily and comfortably, as in a deep sleep . . . (*Pause*)
. . . Keep on relaxing the muscles of your chest . . . Let
them go . . . Let the tension out . . . (*Ten-second pause*)

Now concentrate on each part as I mention it . . .
Abdomen relaxed . . . Back relaxed . . . Chest relaxed . . .
All the tension out . . . (*Pause*)

And now the muscles of your fingers, arms, and shoulders . . . Make a tight fist with each hand . . . Keep your
elbows stiff and straight . . . Elbows stiff and straight as
rods . . . Raise your arms from the shoulders to a forty-
five-degree angle . . . The angle of your arms is halfway
between the couch and vertical . . . Now feel the tension
. . . Study the tension . . . Study the tension in your fingers
. . . in your forearms . . . in your arms and your shoulders
. . . Hold the tension for ten seconds . . . Hold it . . .
Hold it . . . Tense . . . tense . . . tense . . .

And now relax . . . Fingers open . . . Arms down to
sides . . . Just relax . . . Relax the muscles of your fingers
. . . Let them go . . . Relax the muscles of your forearms
Let them go . . . Relax the muscles of your upper arms
. . . Let them go . . . And now the muscles of your shoulders . . . Let them go . . . (*Pause*) . . . Fingers relaxed
. . . arms relaxed . . . shoulders relaxed . . . Let your
arms feel limp and heavy . . . Just keep letting go . . .
(*Ten-second pause*)

And now the muscles between the shoulder blades and
the muscles of your neck . . . Pull your shoulders back
until your shoulder blades are almost touching . . . At the
same time arch your neck until your chin points to the ceil-
ing . . . These are areas very sensitive to nervous tension . . .
Many people feel most of their tension here . . . Feel the
tension . . . Not so tight that it hurts . . . Study the tension
. . . Let it build up . . . (*Ten-second pause*)

Now relax . . . Relax the muscles between your shoulder
blades . . . Let the tension flow out . . . Let it go . . . And

225

relax the muscles of your neck . . . Let them go . . . Your neck muscles are not supporting your head . . . Your head is falling limply against the pillow . . . All the tension out . . . Feel it flowing out . . . (*Thirty-second pause*)

And now the muscles of the upper part of your face . . . Make a grimace with the top part of your face . . . Squeeze your eyes tight shut . . . Wrinkle your nose . . . Frown . . . Notice where you feel the tension . . . Study it . . . Note that you feel the tension in the forehead, between the eyebrows, in the cheeks below the eyes . . .

Now relax . . . let all the tension out . . . Just concentrate on relaxing the muscles of your forehead . . . Let them go . . . Relax your eyelids . . . As they relax you note they begin to feel heavy . . . They make you feel drowsy but you're not going to sleep . . . You must stay alert . . . Relax the muscles at the bridge of your nose . . . Let them go . . . Relax the muscles of your cheeks . . . Remember where they felt tight . . . Let them go . . . (*Ten-second pause*)

And now the muscles of your jaws and tongue . . . Bite hard with your back teeth, press them together until your jaws are tight . . . Feel the tension at your temples, by your ears . . . Wherever you feel the tension, study it . . . Push your tongue against the back of your lower front teeth . . . Your jaws are tight . . . Your tongue is tight . . . Study the tension . . . Get to know it . . . Learn the feel of the tension . . . Hold it, hold it . . . (*Ten- second pause*)

Now relax. Relax the muscles of your jaws . . . Let them go . . . Relax your tongue . . . Your teeth should be slightly parted . . . Your jaw is hanging slack . . . More and more relaxed . . . (*Thirty-second pause*)

Now the muscles around the lower part of your face . . . Tense the muscles around your mouth and chin . . . The best way to make them tense is to grin . . . A big grin, a grimace . . . Draw back your lips to show your teeth, upper and lower teeth . . . Draw the corners of your mouth wide, pull them back and down . . . Feel the tension in your lips, around your mouth, in your chin . . . Let the tension build up . . . Hold it . . . feel it . . . study it . . . Tense . . . tense . . . tense . . . (*Ten-second pause*)

Now relax . . . Relax the muscles around your mouth and chin . . . Let them go . . . Get all the tension out . . . (*Thirty-second pause*) . . . Now try to relax the muscles of your throat . . . Relax the soft part of your throat . . . Relax the soft part of your throat where you swallow . . . Relax the muscles of your voice box . . . Just try to get all the tension out of there . . . (*Thirty-second pause*) That's the end of the first part of the exercise . . . Keep your eyes closed; you're still relaxing.

Now for the second part. Just ask yourself: Is there any tension in my legs, in my thighs, in my buttocks? If there is, let it go . . . Try to get all the tension out . . . More and more relaxed . . . (*Ten-second pause*) Then ask yourself: Is there any tension in my abdomen, my back, or my chest? If there is, let it go . . . Breathe easily and comfortably, the way you do in a deep sleep . . . All the tension out . . . (*Ten-second pause*) And now ask yourself: Is there any tension in my fingers, my arms, or my shoulders? . . . If there is, let it go . . . Let your arms get limp and heavy . . . (*Ten-second pause*) Now ask yourself: Is there any tension between my shoulder blades or in my neck? If there is, let it go . . . Your head is falling limply back to the pillow . . . (*Pause*) . . . And now ask yourself: Is there any tension in my face, my jaws, or my throat? If there is let it go . . . All the tension out . . . Just keep letting go. (*Pause*)

And now the third part of the exercise. Picture your pleasant scene, the scene we discussed before, or if you have trouble with that, picture the word CALM . . . Get a good clear picture, not just the sight, but the sounds, the smells, and the feel . . . If your mind wanders, always bring it back to the pleasant scene. And while you hold that picture in mind, concentrate on relaxing the muscles of your toes . . . Let them go . . . (*Pause*) Relax the muscles of your thighs . . . Let them go . . . (*Pause*) . . . Relax the muscles of your buttocks . . . Let them go . . . (*Pause*) . . . Keep picturing your pleasant scene. If stray thoughts come into your mind, just tell yourself STOP. Put them away . . . Just concentrate on the muscles of your abdomen . . . Let them go . . . Relax . . . (*Pause*) . . . Relax the muscles of your chest . . . Breathe easily and comfortably . . . Keep picturing your pleasant scene . . . (*Pause*) . . . Relax the muscles of your fingers . . . Let them go . . . (*Pause*) . . . Relax your forearms . . . (*Pause*) Relax the muscles of your shoulders . . . Let them go . . . (*Pause*) . . . Relax the muscles of your shoulder blades . . . Let them go . . . . (*Pause*) . . . Relax the muscles of your neck . . . Let them go . . . (*Pause*) . . . Keep picturing the pleasant scene . . . Relax the muscles of your forehead . . . Let them go . . . (*Pause*) . . . Relax your eyelids . . . (*Pause*) . . . Relax the muscles at the bridge of your nose . . . Let them go . . . (*Pause*) . . . Relax your jaw muscles . . . Relax your tongue . . . Relax the muscles around your mouth and chin . . . Let them go . . . (*Pause*) . . . Relax the muscles of your throat . . . All the tension out . . . Let yourself feel limp and heavy all over . . . Now keep picturing the pleasant scene . . . Calm and relaxed . . . Calm and relaxed . . . (*Ten-second pause*) . . . If you feel tension anywhere, just let it go . . . (*Thirty-second pause*) . . . Now I'm going to count from three to one. At the count of one you will sit up and open your eyes. You'll be alert and wide awake and very refreshed . . . Three . . . two . . . one.

APPENDIX B

Fear Inventory

Below are sample items selected from various fear survey schedules. While most of these items involve other people, the usual professional fear inventory includes a much wider range of stimuli. Each stimulus listed here may cause fear or other unpleasant feelings. A check in the appropriate column after each item indicates the extent to which the fear is currently experienced. Space is provided at the end of this schedule so that the individual may add other stimuli. No numerical score is kept, but the schedule provides the behavior therapist with a valuable diagnostic aid. The results are used qualitatively, to determine which fears may be related to the individual's symptoms or problems.

	NONE	LITTLE	SOME	MUCH
1. Angry people				
2. Loud voices				
3. Being teased				
4. Losing control				
5. Strange places				
6. Being alone				

	NONE	LITTLE	SOME	MUCH
7. Sexual organs				
8. Being ignored				
9. Being rejected				
10. Being criticized				
11. Looking foolish				
12. Members of the opposite sex				
13. Nude people				
14. Speaking in public				
15. Making mistakes				
16. Failure				
17. Tough-looking people				
18. Masturbation				
19. Being touched				
20. Becoming mentally ill				
21. Deformed people				
22. Taking responsibility				
23. Sexual inadequacy				
24. Sight of fighting				
25. Feeling angry				

APPENDIX C
Assertion Inventory

These questions provide the behavior therapist with a beginning in his search for areas of assertive difficulties. Questions may be answered with Never (N), Sometimes (S), Often (O), Always (A), or they may be simply answered with Yes or No. There is no score but each item may be used for further investigation or as part of an assertion-training program.

1. Do you complain about poor service in a restaurant?
2. Do you buy things you do not really want because it it difficult to say no to the salesman?
3. Do you hesitate to return items to stores even when there is a good reason for doing so?
4. Do you protest aloud when someone pushes into line in front of you?
5. If someone is talking during a movie, play, or concert, do you ask him to be quiet?
6. Can you begin a conversation with a stranger?
7. If someone "stole" your parking space, would you say or do something?
8. Can you criticize a subordinate? A friend?
9. Can you praise a subordinate? A friend?
10. When a friend makes an unreasonable request, are you able to refuse?
11. Do you keep quiet to avoid hurting people's feelings?
12. Is the goal of keeping things peaceful more important

to you than expressing your opinions and feelings?
13. Do you feel that people take unfair advantage of you or push you around?
14. Do you avoid domineering or bossy people?
15. Do you have difficulty finding things to talk about during a conversation?
17. Do you appropriately show annoyance or anger to men? To women?
18. Can you express tender feelings (liking, affection, love) to men? To women?
19. Is there someone with whom you can discuss very personal matters?
20. When it is appropriate, can you tell your boss or supervisor that you disagree with him?

GLOSSARY

ANXIETY: The subjective experience of disrupted behavior; involves activity of the autonomic nervous system which can be measured by the *galvanic skin response* (see below) or other indications, such as pulse rate.

ASSERTION: The action of declaring oneself; of stating, This is who I am, what I think and feel; characterizes an active rather than a passive approach to life. Lack of assertion is usually characterized by moodiness, low self-esteem, feeling (or actually being) abused.

ASSERTIVE BEHAVIOR: Self-expression through open and direct, honest, and appropriate social communication. Can be taught; *behavior rehearsal* and *feeling talk* (see below) are among the methods used in assertive training.

ASSERTIVE INVENTORY: A systematic survey used by behavior therapists to evaluate assertive behavior. Although a sample inventory appears in the appendix, no really good inventory has yet been devised.

AVERSIVE THERAPY: Method of treatment by which an undesired behavior pattern is associated with an unpleasant or painful experience in order to minimize or eliminate the unwanted behavior.

AVERSIVE STIMULUS: An unpleasant or painful stimulus used in aversive therapy; usually electric shocks to the fingers or forearms, but sometimes chemicals, foghorns, shouts, and even images (see *thought stopping* and *covert sensitization* below).

AVOIDANCE RESPONSE: An act aimed at avoiding anxiety or other unpleasant consequences; an important component in aversive therapy.

BEHAVIOR REHEARSAL: A method of assertive training in which a person role-plays a social situation and performs a desired (i.e., an assertive) act; teaches desired behavior and reduces anxiety in the real-life performance of the act.

BOOSTER SHOCKS: A brief refresher course of aversion therapy given when undesired behavior reappears, which it sometimes does, particularly if it has been impossible to supply strong alternate behaviors for the undesired behavior.

CLASSICAL CONDITIONING: Concepts and methods of the conditioned response originally formulated by Pavlov; basis of *systematic desensitization* (see below).

CONDITIONED RESPONSE: A biological mechanism, developed through evolution, that allows an animal or person to adjust to a constantly changing environment by modifying behavior patterns; may influence biological functions, such as heartbeat, as well as social acts and emotional states. Most psychological difficulties stem from acquisition of incorrect conditioned reflexes.

COVERT SENSITIZATION: An aversive technique using imagery rather than actual stimuli. A person first pictures himself performing the undesired act, then associates it with extremely unpleasant feelings. This association causes the behavior to decrease and disappear in the life situation.

DESENSITIZATION: The process of removing the fear, anxiety, or other unpleasant feeling associated with a given stimulus, usually by pairing the feared stimulus with a reaction that counters fear.

DESENSITIZATION, "IN VIVO": Desensitization in the real-life situation by encountering the feared stimulus under conditions that tend to reduce fear. Eating, drinking, watching movies while in flight, often tend to bring about an *in vivo* desensitization of the fear of flying. This is the method most people spontaneously use to overcome their own fears or the fears of their children.

DESENSITIZATION, SYSTEMATIC: A method of desensitization in which the greatest anxiety or fear is approached gradually by arranging the stimuli in a *hierarchy* (see below) according to the amount of disturbance they elicit. The stimuli are paired with counteranxiety reactions until they no longer elicit any disturbance at all.

EXTINCTION: A progressive decline in the frequency of a given behavior or response. In classical conditioning, when stimuli are no longer paired, the response to the conditioned stimulus tends to extinguish or disappear. In operant conditioning, a response is extinguished when the reinforcements or rewards that maintain that behavior are removed.

FEAR SURVEY SCHEDULE: A systematic survey of the stimuli that evoke fear or other disturbed feelnigs in a person; serves as a basis for beginning treatment. A sample form is shown in the appendix.

FEELING TALK: Direct, honest, and appropriate expression of what a person feels; one method of teaching people to be more assertive.

FLOODING: Treatment (usually through imagery) to extinguish a disturbed reaction to a given situation by causing a person to experience the most anxiety-provoking aspects of the feared situation and prolonging this experience; because it may have some undesirable effects, it is used sparingly.

GALVANIC SKIN RESPONSE (GSR): Slight increase in sweating, due to anxiety, which lowers skin resistance to the flow of electricity; when a very weak current is passed along the skin, the changes are registered on a dial. Basis of the lie detector; also used by behavior therapists to detect changes in anxiety levels.

GENERALIZATION: Universalization of a response to a specific stimulus to an entire class of stimuli with some common characteristic. Fear of an elevator may generalize to all elevators and to trains, airplanes, small rooms, even to certain confining aspects of social relations.

GUIDED IMAGERY: Description of an event for a person who cannot visualize it because he has never experienced it or because it evokes so much anxiety that it has been avoided even in imagination; pictures all feelings, body sensations, and outside stimuli experienced in the actual situation.

HIERARCHY: A series of anxiety-provoking stimuli arranged in ascending order according to the degree of disturbance they evoke; used in systematic desensitization.

IMPLOSIVE THERAPY: A method similar to flooding, but with a wider range of stimuli; patient is instructed to picture most extreme form of disturbing situation and hold it until panic reaction passes; used with caution.

MODELING: A method of vicarious learning by observing another person perform the act; powerful method for learning new skills as well as new emotional reactions and attitudes.

NEUROSIS: A series of learned patterns of maladaptive behavior usually involving high levels of emotional disturbance associated with inappropriate stimuli.

OPERANT CONDITIONING: A powerful method for modifying behavior by systematically controlling consequences of a person's acts; depending on the kind of consequences, or reinforcements, the original behavior may increase or decrease.

OPERANT LEVEL: The base line for measuring change in behavior brought about through operant conditioning, determined by the frequency with which the behavior in question occurs before training or treatment begins.

PHOBIA: Fear, anxiety, or any other disturbed persistent feeling inappropriately evoked by a stimulus or a given class of stimuli.

PSYCHOSIS: Disturbed behavior marked by severe difficulty in correctly evaluating reality; mounting evidence that biological dysfunction may be the cause. Psychotic patients may show neurotic behavior as well. Behavior therapy does not claim to be able to treat the primary psychotic conditions, but it can modify behavior substantially, usually with operant techniques.

REINFORCEMENT: In classical conditioning, the continued pairing of given stimuli with a given response. In systematic desensitization, repeated presentation of anxiety-provoking stimulus under no-anxiety conditions, to strengthen association of stimulus with no anxiety. In operant conditioning, the consequence of an act, which may either increase or decrease the probability of that act's being performed again. Must be immediate and contingent on the behavior being conditioned.

REINFORCEMENT, COVERT: Training, carried out in the imagination, to establish a given behavior pattern. Pattern is broken down into discrete steps, each of which is pictured in the imagination, and is immediately followed by visualization of a positive reinforcement.

REINFORCEMENT, NEGATIVE: Unpleasant, noxious, or painful (punishment) consequence of an act, leading to a decrease in the performance of the act; suppression rather than extinction of the behavior.

REINFORCEMENT, POSITIVE: Reward immediately following a given act; increases the probability of that act's being repeated.

REINFORCEMENT, SOCIAL: Smiles, nods, hugs, words, which serve to maintain or increase the frequency of the behavior that immediately precedes their expression; most common type of reinforcement.

REINFORCEMENT, WITHDRAWAL OF: Total removal or withdrawal of reward to extinguish given behavior; less than total withdrawal makes behavior more resistant to extinction.

REINFORCERS: Objects or acts immediately following a given behavior which cause a change in the frequency of the behavior.

RELAXATION: State of minimal tension and disturbed activity of the autonomic nervous system; often used as a direct treatment for behaviors stemming from tension (e.g., insomnia), or as counter-anxiety response in systematic desensitization.

RESPONSE: Reaction of a person to a stimulus. Called an elicited response when antecedent stimulus is known; called overt response if observable; called covert response if invisible (e.g., a thought).

SHAPING: Step-by-step modification of behavior pattern somewhat similar to desired pattern in order to establish desired behavior; used when desired behavior cannot be positively reinforced because the person does not or cannot initially perform the desired behavior.

STIMULUS: An object or event which influences behavior through the sense organs. Immediately preceding a given behavior, called an antecedent stimulus; anxiety-provoking and counteranxiety stimuli either evoke or inhibit anxiety; immediately following an act, called a reinforcement.

SUD SCALE: Acronym for Subjective Units of Disturbance, used to estimate amount of disturbance experienced by the person; scale ranges from 0 (complete absence of disturbance) to 100 (complete tension).

SYMPTOM: Pattern of maladapted or inappropriate acts, feelings, or thoughts. (Because the term has taken on connotations of deep underlying processes, behavior therapists do not use this term. My own use of it in this book is due to my own prior conditioning.)

TENSION: The physical counterpart of anxiety, usually expressed in tightness of the voluntary muscles.

THOUGHT STOPPING: Method for controlling obsessive thoughts by using a strong, distracting stimulus such as a shout or other loud noise.

"TIME OUT": Method of withdrawing reinforcement in order to extinguish a given behavior which is so disruptive that it cannot be ignored and hence may be reinforced by the attention it receives; disruptive person isolated from all reinforcers.

TOKEN ECONOMY: Form of positive reinforcement, most often used in institutional settings, to strengthen a given behavior. When reinforcement cannot be given immediately after the desired behavior occurs, patient receives tokens, which can later be exchanged for other reinforcers (privileges and even necessities such as meals and beds).

SUGGESTED READING

Baker, Bruce L., Kahn, Michael, and Weiss, Jay M., "Treatment of Insomnia by Relaxation Training," *Journal of Abnormal Psychology,* Vol. 73, No. 6 (1968).

Franks, C. M., *Behavior Therapy: Appraisal and Status,* New York, McGraw-Hill, 1969.

> A rigorous, exceptionally clear, scientific appraisal of research into various behavioral-treatment methods.

Hilgarde, E. R., and Bower, G. H., *Theories of Learning,* 3d ed., New York, Appelton-Century-Crofts, 1966.

> Fairly technical but comprehensive survey of Pavlov's classical conditioning and Skinner's operant conditioning as well as other approaches to the psychology of learning.

Jacobson, Edmund, *Progressive Relaxation,* Chicago, University of Chicago Press, 1938.

Lazarus, Arnold A., "Behavior Therapy in Groups," in G. M. Gazda, ed., *Basic Approaches to Group Psychotherapy and Group Counseling,* Springfield, Illinois, Charles C Thomas, Publisher, 1968.

> Discussion of behavior therapy in general and its practice in groups; also illustrates the treatment of sexual problems and assertive training groups.

Masters, William H., and Johnson, Virginia E., *Human Sexual Inadequacy,* Boston, Little, Brown, 1970.

> Must reading for anyone concerned with sexual problems; authors' clinical approach and training exercises described in detail.

Meacham, M. L., and Wiesen, A. E., *Changing Classroom Behavior: A Manual for Precision Teaching,* Scranton, Pennsylvania, International Textbook Co., 1969.

> Principles of learning that can be applied by the teacher to facilitate learning and improve classroom behavior. Research findings elucidate principles of precision teaching, illustrated by classroom experience.

Patterson, Gerald R., and Gullion, M. Elizabeth, *Living with Children,* Champaign, Illinois, Research Press, 1968.

Rubin, R. D., Fensterheim, H., Lazarus, A. A., and Franks, C. M., *Advances in Behavior Therapy, 1969,* New York, Academic Press, 1971.

> Papers from the proceedings of the national meeting of the Association for the Advancement of Behavior Therapy; good picture of contemporary clinical and research work.

Salter, Andrew, *Conditioned Reflex Therapy,* New York, Farrar, Straus & Giroux, 1949; Capricorn, 1961.

> Has helped more people with problems in assertion than any other book I know. Application of Pavlov's excitation and inhibition concepts to emotional disturbances; many case illustrations; useful exercises. Extremely readable.

Schaefer, H. H., and Martin, P. L., *Behavior Therapy,* New York, McGraw-Hill, 1969.

> In language intelligible to most laymen, authors provide numerous examples, exercises, and practical help for those involved in the treatment of mental patients.

Wolpe, Joseph, *The Practice of Behavior Therapy,* Elmsford, N.Y., Pergamon Press, 1969.

> Probably the basic clinical handbook in behavior therapy; relatively easy to read and understand. Descriptions of systematic desensitization are particularly enlightening.

Ullmann, L. P., and Krasner, L., *Case Studies in Behavior Modification,* New York, Holt, Rinehart & Winston, 1966.

> Case reports of a wide variety reprinted from professional literature, with an excellent introduction to behavior modification. Largely technical, but interesting and rewarding.

———, *A Psychological Approach to Abnormal Behavior,* Englewood Cliffs, N.J., Prentice-Hall, 1969.

> College-level text for a course in abnormal psychology. Many cherished ideas challenged.

Yates, A. S., *Behavior Therapy,* New York, Wiley, 1970.

> Probably the best single book on behavior therapy, although it does not provide detailed descriptions of techniques. Organized by syndromes rather than by methods; covers a wide scope from tics to mental deficiency.